What people are saying about …

EVERYDAY SUPERNATURAL

"Words, works and wonders are all ways in which Jesus put the kingdom of God on display as He walked this earth. As the Church today we're called to follow His example, showcasing the loving reign of God through each of these ways. In reality, 'wonders' often gets less attention than the other expressions, and that's why a book like this is so important. In their brilliantly unique style Mike and Andy show us you don't have to be an expert or a member of the 'spiritually elite' to walk in the everyday supernatural. You just need to have a heart that seeks to listen, and a life that seeks to obey."

Matt Redman, worship songwriter and
recording artist, author of *10,000 Reasons*

"Mike Pilavachi and Andy Croft are ideal guides for anyone wanting to live daily in the power of the Holy Spirit. They are fun, insightful and have an infectious passion for Jesus."

Nicky Gumbel, pioneer of the Alpha Course
and vicar of Holy Trinity Brompton

"Mike and Andy engage with the most exciting and essential of themes with great passion and practical insight. Packed with biblical and personal stories this is a great book for people who want to step out of their comfort zones and step into the adventure of following Christ and being empowered by the Holy Spirit."

Tim Hughes, leader of St. Luke's Gas Street Church and worship recording artist

"The promise of the New Testament is that the Holy Spirit is poured out on everyone. In *Everyday Supernatural,* Mike and Andy provide a practical and accessible guide to living this life in the Spirit. This book has the potential to transform the experience of any believer—highly recommended!"

Roy Godwin, author of *The Grace Outpouring* and *The Way of Blessing*

EVERYDAY SUPERNATURAL

EVERYDAY SUPERNATURAL

Living a Spirit-Led Life
without Being Weird

MIKE PILAVACHI
& ANDY CROFT

David C Cook®

transforming lives together

EVERYDAY SUPERNATURAL
Published by David C Cook
4050 Lee Vance View
Colorado Springs, CO 80918 U.S.A.

Integrity Music Ltd., a subsidiary of David C Cook,
26-28 Lottbridge Drove, Eastbourne, BN23 6NT, UK

The graphic circle C logo is a registered trademark of David C Cook.

The website addresses recommended throughout this book are offered as a
resource to you. These websites are not intended in any way to be or imply an
endorsement on the part of David C Cook, nor do we vouch for their content.

LCCN 2016938481
ISBN 978-0-7814-1499-9
eISBN 978-1-4347-1091-8

© 2016 Michael Pilavachi and Andrew John Croft

The Team: Ian Matthews, Liza Hoeksma, Amy Konyndyk, Nick
Lee, Jon Middel, Helen Macdonald, Susan Murdock
Cover Design: Nick Lee
Cover Photo: Shutterstock

Printed in the United Kingdom
First Edition 2016

1 2 3 4 5 6 7 8 9 10

052616

We dedicate this book to Josiah.
May you light up the world as
you have lit up our lives.
With much love,
Dad and Uncle Mike

CONTENTS

STUDY GUIDE CONTENTS

ACKNOWLEDGEMENTS

We are both conscious that this book would never have been written without the contributions and support of an army of our friends. So, we would like to blame the following:

Liza Hoeksma for her skill, patience and calmness as she has written this book with us. Liza has been part of our church for almost the whole of its twenty-three-year existence so many of our stories are also her stories. Ali Martin and Patrick Sinclair for reading through the drafts and offering much needed suggestions. David and Mary Pytches for their love, support, encouragement and wisdom, not just during the writing of this book but also for many, many years. Matt Redman for coming up with a great book title within minutes of being asked. That man has a way with words. Richard and Prue Bedwell for being so faithful both in your devotion to the Lord and in your friendship and encouragement of us over many years. Taylor Grieg, our wonderful PA, for regularly juggling our diaries so we could write together. Joe Cook for tirelessly transcribing many of our talks and reading through various drafts. Ian Matthews of David C Cook, who has been so patient even when we have regularly missed deadlines, and Jennie Pollock for all her help in editing the manuscript. Les and Judith Moir who have been encouragers for more years than we care to remember. Blaine Cook who has taught us so much about these things not only in his teaching but even more by his example.

Andy would like to thank Beth and Josiah for all the grace they have shown while he has been locked in his study for hours on end. Mike would like to thank his goldfish who have sometimes not been fed as Mike was distracted trying to figure out how to use Word documents on his MacBook Air.

Any book like this is written in community so we would both like to thank the kind and gracious people of Soul Survivor Watford, the church that we love and love to serve. Finally, all the passionate, exuberant, expectant, cheeky and fun-loving young people and young adults who have attended Soul Survivor and Momentum conferences over the years. We have been on an amazing journey together; the adventure continues.

INTRODUCTION

Then Moses said, "Now show me your glory."
Exodus 33:18

Mike

Over the years I have had many airport disasters. Once I arrived at Stansted airport to go to Berlin only to discover I'd forgotten my passport. I tried checking in with my driver's licence but they wouldn't accept it. I phoned the Soul Survivor office and my friend Ali rushed to my house, got the passport and drove to the airport.

Unfortunately, Ali arrived just as the plane was leaving. I was so angry with myself and as we were walking dejectedly to the car I noticed a man standing on his own with his suitcase beside him. A little thought flashed through my mind: *That man needs encouragement, go and pray for him.* I generally dismiss those thoughts but this time I made a big mistake: I mentioned it to Ali. To my annoyance she got excited. "This has never happened to me before," she said. "It's like one of those Christian books. Let's go and pray for him!" I tried to assure her that it was just my little thought and said, "I'm fed up; all I want to do is go home." She was too excited to listen. "But what if it's from God?" she said.

In the end I realised I was going to disappoint her if I didn't make an effort. I said, "Okay, let's walk past and see if God says anything else." We walked past. Nothing. We walked past a second time. Still nothing. We walked past that man seven times. In the end, more out of desperation than anything else, I went up to him. "Excuse me, sir, we're not weird," (he didn't look convinced), "but we think Jesus told us that you need encouragement and we wondered if we could pray for you."

He looked at us in astonishment and said, "I've just arrived in this country to pastor a church in Essex. I've been waiting for two of the elders of the church to collect me but they're late. I've been standing here thinking, 'What on earth have I done? Why am I here?' And I just prayed a little while ago, 'God, I would love it if you would give me some encouragement before they arrive to collect me.'"

I was more amazed than the pastor was! "Are you serious?" I asked. So we prayed for him and went on our way rejoicing. As we drove home talking excitedly about what God had done I couldn't help but think of all the times I've had little thoughts like that and dismissed them. How many times I hadn't taken the risk. How many times I'd thought, *It's just me.*

THE NORMAL CHRISTIAN LIFE

It's possible for all followers of Jesus to see God's supernatural power at work. Not once or twice in a lifetime, but every day.

Just as Mike nearly missed it at the airport, so we all often miss the supernatural because we don't understand that it comes in an everyday, ordinary package. We (Mike and Andy) are utterly convinced that the Bible teaches it should be normal for Christians to hear God speak, to exercise spiritual gifts and to witness in the power of the Holy Spirit. It's something we should expect to happen at airports and bus stops, in our schools and in our workplaces, with our family and with our friends. We are about to begin a journey towards this becoming an everyday occurrence: a new normal.

We don't need to become super-spiritual Christians to see God at work. And we don't need to become weird. We simply need to discover that God wants to break into our "ordinary" with his extra-ordinary power; and we need to learn to say yes!

We hope that as a result of reading this book you will become more equipped and prepared for God to use you. We will talk practically about what it means to be filled with the Spirit. We're going to talk about how to pray in the Spirit, hear God speak and pray for healing. We are also going to look at the importance of obedience, the reality of seeing God's power operating through our weakness and the role of faith in everything.

That which sustains us on any journey is our motivation and our destination. Happily, in this instance both our motivation and our destination are the same; we are driven by, and drawn towards a revelation of God's glory. As we discover the biblical teaching and practical guidance on how to live everyday supernatural lives let us keep this in the front of our minds: the motivation and the destination is the revelation of the glory of God.

THE GLORY OF GOD

Have you ever wondered what God's glory might look like? We usually imagine it to be spectacular. "Holiness", "power" and "majesty" are three words often associated with glory. Whilst this is true, we'd suggest there are three other words that are even more foundational. This is something Moses discovered. Towards the end of his life Moses was talking with God and made an incredible request: "Then Moses said, 'Now show me your glory'" (Exod. 33:18). We could be forgiven for saying to him, "Moses, aren't you a little greedy?" If there was anyone who had seen the glory of God surely it was Mo! God had spoken to him out of a burning bush. He'd seen God cover Egypt with plagues of frogs and locusts, the Nile turned to blood and even the sun blotted out. Moses had seen a sea part, manna fall from heaven and water spring from a rock. Every morning he'd been led by a pillar of cloud and every evening by a pillar of burning fire. He'd received the Ten Commandments and spoken with God face to face.

What more could Moses have asked for? Perhaps for the Lord to part the Pacific Ocean? Maybe a ten-year supply of San Pellegrino on tap? Did he want strawberry cheesecake to fall out of the sky every day? Surely, there was nothing left to see!

However, God's response tells us everything:

> And the LORD said, "I will cause all my goodness to pass in front of you, and I will proclaim my name, the LORD, in your presence. I will have mercy on whom I will have mercy, and I will have compassion on whom I will have compassion." (Exod. 33:19)

The three key words here are *goodness, mercy* and *compassion.*
God's glory is spectacular but not always in the flashing-lights-fire-
in-the-sky way we might expect. When he reveals his glory to Moses
he is revealing power but not for its own sake. Rather, God's power
reveals his spectacular love. In the end God's glory is his character. A
true revelation of God's glory, a genuine miracle, a real act of supernatural power will cause us to wonder afresh at his character—his
goodness, mercy and compassion. A life full of the everyday supernatural is a life full of acts of divine power that reveal more of God's
love. As we grow in these things, we will marvel not just at the little
everyday miracles we begin to witness, but much more at the mercy
of our God who cares for people when they least expect it and most
need it.

THE POWERFUL LOVE OF JESUS

If there's anyone who revealed the truth of this, it is Jesus, the Glory
of God made flesh. Thousands of years after Moses asked to see the
glory, John wrote, "We have seen his glory, the glory of the one and
only Son, who came from the Father, full of grace and truth" (John
1:14). When Jesus walked the earth incredible power flowed through
him. It was a power that saw lepers cleansed, storms calmed, demons
driven away, blind eyes opened and the dead raised. But it is possible to read about these things and miss the people whose lives were
transformed.

The result of Jesus's miracles wasn't simply that people were
awed. They were loved. Think about it. Blind people would have seen
their families and the world for the first time. Those who had been

outcasts, despised and rejected, were made whole and welcomed in. Those who were burying their relatives discovered they needed to postpone the funeral. Even badly planned wedding receptions were rescued!

Time and again we are told that Jesus was motivated by compassion. Lame beggars, sinful women, people who were hungry and poor, people who were frightened and alone, and people who were trapped and desperate all met the Glory of God. Their lives were transformed because they found him to be full of goodness, mercy and compassion. They encountered a power that revealed the love of God and were changed forever.

OUR HOPE

Believe it or not, this is what is meant to happen when people meet us! As Jesus's disciples we are to follow him—doing the things he did. Of course this means feeding the hungry, loving the lonely and sharing the gospel. It also means doing the miraculous works of Jesus. He encourages us to expect the supernatural in and through our everyday lives:

> Very truly I tell you, whoever believes in me will do the works I have been doing, and they will do even greater things than these, because I am going to the Father. And I will do whatever you ask in my name, so that the Father may be glorified in the Son. You may ask me for anything in my name, and I will do it. (John 14:12–14)

These "works" of Jesus are called "signs and wonders". They signposted people to God's love. And they caused them to wonder: "There is a God and this is what he's like."

As we begin to seek a life full of the everyday supernatural, as we aim to grow into the normal Christian life, let us write 1 Corinthians 13:1–3 on our heart:

> If I speak in the tongues of men or of angels, but do not have love, I am only a resounding gong or a clanging cymbal. If I have the gift of prophecy and can fathom all mysteries and all knowledge, and if I have a faith that can move mountains, but do not have love, I am nothing. If I give all I possess to the poor and give over my body to hardship that I may boast, but do not have love, I gain nothing.

We can prophesy till the cows come home, we can perform healings that put pharmacies out of business, we can see miracles that would make Elijah envious, but unless we make love our aim we haven't a hope of revealing the glory of God to others.

As you begin to practise the principles in this book you can expect God to begin speaking to you. You can expect him to heal people through you. You can expect to pray in tongues and you can expect to grow in faith. In fact, you should expect to see a new level of God's power in all your interactions—at church, at home and on the streets. But we want you to know what you should *really expect* as you begin to move in these things. You will see the glory of God, and by that we mean the goodness, mercy and compassion of God. A power that reveals amazing love. As Mike and Ali drove home from the airport that day they were rejoicing, not only because they caught a small glimpse of God's power, but much more because they encountered his overwhelming kindness.

Let's journey together into the normal Christian life, the everyday supernatural.

Now, God, show us your glory …

1

THE POWER IS IN THE PRESENCE

*If your Presence does not go with us, do not send us up
from here.... What else will distinguish me and your people
from all the other people on the face of the earth?*

Exodus 33:15, 16

Hopefully you are reading this book because you long to see God do
miracles. You want to hear his voice and have prophetic words for
people. You want to see an increase in the supernatural power of God
in your life. So, where do we begin?

Mike

When I was a student in Birmingham I went to a meeting led by
a famous healing evangelist. He talked a lot about faith and gave
the impression that if you had enough faith you would be healed of
anything.

Sitting a few rows in front of me was a man with no legs. At the culmination of the talk the healing evangelist said, "If you're in a wheelchair get up now—by faith—and start to walk." I watched as this man's two friends hoisted him by his arms from the wheelchair. He started to frantically move his stumps until he was red in the face. I could see him sweating and becoming more and more exhausted; he was giving it his all but his legs didn't grow. Eventually his two friends put him back in his wheelchair and wandered off, embarrassed.

The meeting came to an end. Everyone headed for the exits and I stayed there watching. The man sat in his wheelchair trying to recover his breath and staring into space. After a while he shrugged his shoulders and started to wheel himself away. I vowed at that moment that I would never have anything to do with a ministry as ugly as that. And I would never treat anyone in such a cruel way. To this day I regret not going up to that man, giving him a hug and telling him that God loves him very much.

———————

As we look to see God move in increasing power our starting place needs to be understanding the connection between God's power and God's love. What happened at that meeting in Birmingham was deeply flawed. There may have been some power in the meeting, but there was no love. Can you imagine Jesus doing something like that to anyone? We can't. Praying for healing should have drawn that man towards God; instead he was left feeling abandoned by him. The last thing we want to do is to move in more power and less love. We can both avoid this mistake *and* see God move in increasing power by understanding that what we must seek isn't God's power, it's his presence.

SEEK JESUS FIRST

When we talk about "seeking God's presence" we simply mean we are seeking to be close to Jesus. Our goal should be relationship *with* Jesus, not power *from* Jesus. Christianity isn't complicated. It's not about rules; it's an invitation to have a relationship with God. God's power is never something he sends to us from a distance. Miracles are not like parcels from Amazon, arriving totally disconnected from the sender. The power of God can't be separated from his presence. If you are standing next to a fire you know you'll become warm, if you jump in a pool you know you'll get wet. In the same way, if you are close to the Lord his power will be present. The power is in the presence. And when we seek to be close to God the potential for the supernatural is all around us.

THE POWER IS IN THE PRESENCE

Here are a few stories to illustrate what we mean.

Mike

Some years ago I was in a prayer and worship meeting and found myself sitting next to a very elderly lady. We were singing Psalm 134 and everyone was clapping. As the song came to an end, everyone stopped clapping except the old lady. After a few moments she realised she was the only one and stopped as well. She then told the group what had happened. She'd been suffering from arthritis for the past few years—her hands had been so twisted she hadn't even been able to hold a coffee cup. She said, "I haven't clapped for years, and as I was worshipping Jesus I forgot that I couldn't clap. Look," she said, waving her hands, "he healed me when I wasn't looking!"

This lady had sought Jesus; she had longed to be close to him. It's not at all surprising to us that in seeking his presence she encountered his power as well.

Andy

A few summers ago at one of our Soul Survivor events, a young man approached me surrounded by some of his youth group. He had been brought along to Soul Survivor the previous year when he wasn't a Christian. He told me that for most of his life he'd had serious anger problems. When he was seven years old someone had murdered his brother, stabbing him in the chest. Understandably, from that point on this guy had been overwhelmed by anger. He'd ended up in all sorts of trouble; he never fitted in at school and life had become very difficult. Eventually he came across some Christians who brought him along to Soul Survivor.

He told me that for the first four days of the event he hadn't been able to be in the meetings. He kept walking out. He would find a fence post and punch it until his knuckles were raw and bleeding. Then he would come back into the meeting, hiding his hands in his pockets so that nobody would notice. Finally, on the last night of Soul Survivor he came into the meeting and said to God, "If you're real, show me!" He said to me, "God turned up … I know you are meant to enjoy encountering God but I didn't. In some ways it was a horrible experience because I felt like all my anger was being sucked out of me. It was the only emotion I'd ever known and so I didn't know what to do." Then he added, "But I'm changed now." His youth group all smiled and nodded excitedly. "He's so different!" they agreed.

"Since I met with God last year I've been full of peace, and next year I'm going to be an intern at my church. My dream is to eventually bring my own youth group to Soul Survivor."

I met him again last summer. He had his own youth group and his dream had come true. This guy had cried out to Jesus—he had sought and encountered Jesus. God showed up, and when God is present, so is his power.

WHAT REALLY MAKES US DIFFERENT?

When we talk of being "supernatural" we can imagine this to look like wandering around with special powers. Perhaps staring mysteriously at people in the street before predicting the results of the Champions League. But this isn't at all what we mean. Moses understood what really set people apart. Around the same time he said, "Show me your glory," he also said: "If your Presence does not go with us, do not send us up from here … What else will distinguish me and your people from all the other people on the face of the earth?" (Exod. 33:15, 16).

This is a huge statement! Moses knew that Israel could have the best military, the best economy and the best football team but all that would be worthless if they didn't have God's presence. Just as this was true for Moses and Israel it's true for us today. What sets Christians apart from non-Christians isn't that we're funnier, better looking, or better dressed than non-Christians. (Andy claims he's the exception to this rule.) What really distinguishes us is that we are a people of God's presence. It's never been about what we can do—it's about *who we are with*.

Some Christians do experience more of God's supernatural power in their everyday lives than others. We've noticed these don't seem to be Christians who wear white suits or have memorised special techniques. They are simply the people who are looking to be close to God. They are people who, like Moses, are desperate for God's presence in their lives. They won't go anywhere without him!

Andy

Mike has told me for years about a hero of his: Brother Andrew. I've read all of his books and especially loved *God's Smuggler*. Brother Andrew felt God call him to serve in places no one else would go. In the early years of his ministry he would load his car up with Bibles and drive them to communist-controlled Eastern Europe. What he was doing was dangerous but Brother Andrew would pray and God would miraculously "blind" the eyes of the border guards. They would open his car boot, somehow not see the Bibles (which were there in plain sight), and Brother Andrew would be waved through.

God's Smuggler tells of all sorts of everyday supernatural encounters: God helped his car keep going without fuel; he once recognised another believer "in his spirit" as he passed him in the street; he saw miraculous answers to prayer. It sounds crazy, doesn't it? But his life has been full of God's power.

Brother Andrew is now in his eighties and spends his later years visiting drug barons and terrorists in order to show them the love of Jesus. He once cancelled coming to speak at Soul Survivor because he had sneaked across the border into Afghanistan and was baptising a hundred new believers in a river. After reading the books, and hearing Mike's stories, I was thrilled when I got the chance to meet him.

Sitting in his home, looking at photos of Andrew with numerous well-known terrorists with whom he shares the gospel, I asked him a question that had been burning in me for a long time: "Brother Andrew, you are in your old age and you are on fire for Jesus. I'm in my twenties and that's where I want to be when I'm your age. What's your secret?" I was really asking, "How do I get to be like you and see God do all the crazy things you've seen?" Andrew looked at me for a moment and then he said this: "The secret is to stick close to Jesus."

I remember at the time feeling faintly disappointed and thinking, *Really? "Stick close to Jesus"? It can't be that simple.* That was eight years ago now. I've never forgotten that statement and I've been discovering the truth of it every single day.

There is one foundational key to becoming increasingly tuned in to the supernatural; it is pursuing relationship with God and seeking to be close to him.

SEEK "ONE THING"

This sounds so simple we can be tempted to write it off as unimportant. The story of King David shows us otherwise. His was a life full of God's power. God raised him up from being a shepherd boy to being the greatest of Israel's kings. David witnessed miraculous military victories—from slaying the nine-foot Goliath with a stone to defeating all of Israel's enemies. And yet when we read the songs he wrote (recorded in the Psalms) we discover what David was pursuing his entire life—it wasn't military strength, it wasn't supernatural power for its own sake, it was God's presence.

> *One thing* I ask from the LORD,
>   this only do I seek:
> that I may dwell in the house of the LORD
>   all the days of my life,
> to gaze on the beauty of the LORD
>   and to seek him in his temple.
> For in the day of trouble
>   he will keep me safe in his dwelling;
> he will hide me in the shelter of his sacred tent
>   and set me high upon a rock. (Ps. 27:4–5)

The one thing David sought all his days was to be in the presence of God, to sit in the house of God, to gaze on the face of God. This and other psalms record the cries of his heart. He sang with joy:

> Where can I go from your Spirit?
>   Where can I flee from your presence?
> If I go up to the heavens, you are there;
>   if I make my bed in the depths, you are there.
>   (Ps. 139:7–8)

It was God's presence that gave David comfort and strength:

> Even though I walk
>   through the darkest valley,
> I will fear no evil,
>   for you are with me. (Ps. 23:4)

And when he sinned, committing adultery with Bathsheba, he cried out for mercy, begging God,

> Do not cast me from your presence
>   or take your Holy Spirit from me. (Ps. 51:11)

This wasn't something that was unique to David; many other great biblical characters were desperate for his presence. The rest of the Psalms are shot through with similar exhortations:

> How lovely is your dwelling place,
>   LORD Almighty!
> My soul yearns, even faints,
>   for the courts of the LORD;
> my heart and my flesh cry out
>   for the living God. (Ps. 84:1–2)

There's great force in these words—yearning souls, bodies that are crying out.

> As the deer pants for streams of water,
>   so my soul pants for you, my God.

> My soul thirsts for God, for the living God.
> When can I go and meet with God?
> (Ps. 42:1–2)

This image isn't of Bambi prancing around near a forest stream; it's an image from the scorching Middle East. A deer is panting for water; its throat is burning for that which gives it life.

Let's not miss the significance of this. Think about Moses again: one of the great leaders of Israel. He was given the Law, led Israel through the Red Sea and saw manna fall from heaven. *He* knew that the key was God's presence. David—the greatest king Israel ever had—battle-scarred and hardened by a life of war, wept and cried out for the presence of God. He could have sought God for a great army or great wealth but left us in no doubt that *his one driving ambition* was to be in God's presence. David's determination was shared by countless others, both those who wrote Israel's psalms and the tens of thousands who would have sung them.

And today, whenever we meet someone who is being used by God in incredible ways, we realise they are uncompromising in their pursuit of Jesus. They are not seeking power *from* him, but relationship *with* him. They will stop at nothing to be close to him. And they discover a profound secret along the way: the power is in the presence.

GOD IS SEEKING US

If the great heroes of the faith don't impress upon us the importance of God's presence, there is another we can call upon: God himself.

The story of the Bible—from Genesis to Revelation—communicates that God's desire is not only that we might move in supernatural power, it's that we might live a life of intimacy with him. His first concern is to draw us close.

From their creation, Adam and Eve were able to walk in the cool of the day with God. The great consequence of their sin was that they separated themselves from God and one another. They hid from him. This is why the first question God ever had to ask was, "Where are you?" (Gen. 3:9). The human race has been hiding from God's presence ever since.

The rest of the story of the Bible is a story of God seeking to draw people to himself. At the heart of Israel's calling was that they would be a people of God's own possession, that he would live among them. Remember Moses's words, "What else will distinguish us?" In practice this meant God commanded the Israelites to make a home for him. It started as the tabernacle (a tent) and it later became the temple. We can read about some of God's preferences for furniture, room sizes and the way that the priests should dress and smell in Exodus 25–40. At first reading it can seem a little bizarre. Why was God so particular?

Andy

Not long after I started dating my wife, Beth, she "invited" me to go shopping with her. Whilst on the shopping trip, it was "suggested" to me that I might want to buy one or two new T-shirts (the ones that she picked out). Some time later Beth gave me a new aftershave for my birthday. I was told I should show my gratitude for the gift by wearing it every day. A short time later I was instructed to begin paying more than £5 for my haircuts. I did exactly as I was told. A smarter shirt, a better fragrance and a sharper haircut later, I'm happily married.

Andy's wife made it very clear that if he was to be seen in her presence it was best for him to look, sound and smell exactly as she wanted. Whilst we in no way want to suggest that God is like a girlfriend, he did make similar demands to the people of Israel. He wanted to say to them, "If you are to be in my presence you need to understand that I'm holy, and by doing these things you recognise the relationship has to be on my terms." It may sound like hard work for Israel, but they received an unimaginable blessing: God moved in among them in a very real way. His glory filled the Holy of Holies, the inner most room of the tabernacle and later the temple (2 Chron. 6–7). This became his home, his address on earth. He was close.

Unsurprisingly, when God was close so was his blessing. So long as Israel devoted themselves to relationship with him and honoured his presence they experienced the shalom (or "wholeness"), of God. Sadly, however, they repeated the sin of Adam and Eve. They regularly chose independence from God. Throughout the Old Testament we see this happening again and again and eventually God withdrew his presence. When his presence left, so did his blessing. Jerusalem was destroyed, Israel was exiled to Babylon and although they eventually returned and rebuilt the temple there is no account of God's presence returning. God's ambition is that we might live in his presence. Israel spectacularly spurned his offer. But God is very determined ...

EMMANUEL—"GOD WITH US."

Despite Israel distancing themselves from him, God didn't walk away. Astonishingly, he came even closer. Enter Jesus. "The Word became flesh and blood, and moved into the neighborhood" (John 1:14 THE MESSAGE). It's easy to miss the magnitude of what John is saying here. The presence that dwelled in the tabernacle and the temple was born of a virgin and literally lived among normal people like us. The walking, shaving, eating, preaching, saving Holy of Holies.

Again, when God was present so was his blessing. Jesus gave himself certain names: "I am the way and the truth and the life" (John 14:6). He didn't say "I give life" or "I point to the way" but "I *am* the life" and "I *am* the way." We receive life by being close to him.

That which might sound like abstract theory became a concrete reality for those who met Jesus. They found that in drawing near to him they had drawn near to life itself. Take the paralysed man whose friends made a hole in a roof and lowered him right in front of Jesus (Mark 2:1–12). When he landed at Jesus's feet he first of all found total forgiveness, and then complete healing for his legs. To be near Jesus is to be healed, body, mind and soul, because Jesus is life.

When Jesus was born he was given the title "Emmanuel", which means "God with us". After he rose from the dead, as he was about to ascend to heaven, he said to his disciples, "Surely I am *with you* always, to the very end of the age" (Matt. 28:20). It was the cross that made this possible. On the cross Jesus cried out, "My God, my God, why have you abandoned me?" (Matt. 27:46 NLT). He took on our sin and as a result was cut off from God the Father. Jesus was separated from the Father for a moment in eternity so that for all eternity we never will be. There is now "no condemnation for those who are in Christ Jesus," and nothing "in all creation, will be able to separate us from the love of God that is in Christ Jesus our Lord" (Rom. 8:1, 39). God's Son experienced the momentary darkness of separation, that we might know the eternal light of God's presence. With Adam and Eve we went into hiding, on the cross Jesus found us. We never need to hide again.

GOD WITHIN US

So, this leaves us with the question, "How is Jesus present with us now?" The answer is by his Holy Spirit. Before Jesus went to the cross he made this remarkable promise, "And I will ask the Father, and he will give you another advocate to help you and be with you forever— the Spirit of truth" (John 14:16–17). The unique, only begotten Son of God is promising another like him!

Jesus was referring to the Holy Spirit, "The world cannot accept him, because it neither sees him nor knows him. But you know him, for *he lives with you and will be in you*" (John 14:17). It is through the Holy Spirit that Jesus comes to live inside us. This is something that should stagger us. Paul couldn't get over it; he made it his life's goal to share "the mystery that has been kept hidden for ages and generations, but is now disclosed to the Lord's people.

To them God has chosen to make known among the Gentiles the glorious riches of this mystery, which is Christ in you, the hope of glory" (Col. 1:26–27).

The great secret Paul is talking about—the one that has been kept hidden for hundreds of years—is not Christ beside us. It's not Christ near us. It's Christ within us.

The key to living a life full of supernatural power is to understand that the power is in the presence. As we are close to Jesus so we will see him move in us and through us.

The power is in the presence.

And his presence is in us.

2

BEING FILLED WITH THE SPIRIT

How much more will your Father in heaven give
the Holy Spirit to those who ask him!

Luke 11:13

LIVING TEMPLES

Some years ago the two of us travelled to Israel for the first time. We loved visiting all the places we had read about for years. We walked the old Roman road to Emmaus. Andy wandered across as much of it as he could to maximise the chance he would stand in the exact same spot as the risen Jesus. We went to the valley where David fought Goliath and both collected five smooth stones. (Mike is convinced one of his has a bit of blood on it.)

One of the highlights was our visit to the old city of Jerusalem and particularly to what is known as the Wailing Wall where Jews have prayed for hundreds of years. Every crack in the bleached yellow stones is crammed with tiny scrunched up balls of paper—the scribbled prayers of visitors. Jews go there to pray for the coming of the promised Messiah; it was here, after all, that God's presence dwelt thousands of years ago. As the two of us approached the wall, saw the scores of people knelt in prayer, and reflected on where we were, it struck us that we were entering somewhere holy. We thought to ourselves, "How utterly amazing, Almighty God lived here, in this very place. This was where the ark of the covenant was. This is where the Glory fell." And then it hit us: "And now he lives in us."

As Christians we believe something astonishing. We say this with all humility: God lives in Mike Pilavachi and God lives in Andy Croft. We are his holy temple, his home. Jesus tells us, "Anyone who loves me will obey my teaching. My Father will love them, and we will come to them and make our home with them" (John 14:23). This is why Paul wrote to the church in Corinth, "Don't you know that you yourselves are God's temple and that God's Spirit dwells in your midst?" (1 Cor. 3:16). To become a Christian isn't to tick a box next to a set of beliefs, it's to enter into a relationship with the living God. As we do this the living God pours his Spirit into us.

DO I HAVE THE HOLY SPIRIT?

This is a question Christians often ask. Behind the question is a wondering, "If I haven't had a dramatic encounter with the Spirit, if he hasn't met me in an interesting or obvious way, then have I really got the Holy Spirit?" You may have been in a meeting where other people have shaken, fallen down or prayed in tongues, and nothing has happened to you. Do you have the Spirit?

Andy

I remember seeing the Holy Spirit move in power for the first time when I was a very new Christian. I was at a meeting praying for someone with a friend, and after a few minutes the guy just fell over! Fortunately Mike (who I didn't know at that point) was leading the meeting and was reassuring people, explaining that it was nothing to worry about. My friend and I probably should have knelt down to continue to pray for the guy on the floor but instead we started arguing about whose prayer had made him fall over!

Over the next few years, I saw all sorts happen when the Holy Spirit was invited. Some of it, of course, may have just been people getting excited, but much of it was God. People were transformed and healed in powerful encounters. I spoke to them afterwards and it seemed amazing what had happened. It didn't seem to happen to me though. To this day I've never fallen over and I've never shaken. Not even a little bit! After a while I began to wonder, "What's wrong with me? Why does God seem to meet everybody except me?"

If you are asking, "Do I have the Holy Spirit?" we want to answer you clearly: yes, you do. All Christians, whether they have had a dramatic physical encounter or not, have the Spirit living inside of them. This is what the Bible teaches and if you're still wondering, here are a couple of tests you can do:

TEST ONE: WHAT YOU BELIEVE

Writing to the Corinthians, Paul says, "Therefore I want you to know that no one who is speaking by the Spirit of God says, 'Jesus be cursed,' and no one can say, 'Jesus is Lord,' except by the Holy Spirit" (1 Cor. 12:3).

This is a simple but crucial proof of the Spirit's activity. It's not possible to say and *mean*, "Jesus is Lord" except by the Holy Spirit. It is the job of the Holy Spirit to lead people to Jesus. "When the Advocate comes, whom I will send to you from the Father—the Spirit of truth who goes out from the Father—he will testify about me" (John 15:26). This is a sign of him living in you. If you acknowledge Jesus to be your Lord and Saviour, it is because the Spirit is at work within you.

TEST TWO: WHAT YOU DESIRE

To the believers in Rome, Paul wrote, "Those who live according to the flesh have their minds set on what the flesh desires; but those who live in accordance with the Spirit have their minds set on what the Spirit desires" (Rom. 8:5).

A second sign of the Spirit at work in our lives is that we begin to desire what he desires.

The older of our two authors desires one thing above all others. He doesn't really mind if it's Chinese, Mexican, Thai, Lebanese, French or Greek so long as there is plenty of it. During the year Andy was Mike's intern Mike "invested in him". Mainly by taking him to restaurants. Mike is inordinately proud of the fact that

Andy visited more restaurants in that one year than in the rest of his life put together. By the end of the year Andy—and we mean this genuinely—had discovered a new passion for food, one that he never knew he had. He now proudly takes people to the best restaurant in Watford and orders for them—just like Mike.

When you spend time with someone who cares about something deeply—whether it's food, fashion or football—their passion can be contagious. When we are full of the Holy Spirit we begin to care about the things the Spirit cares about. We have "our minds set on what the Spirit desires." Below is a list of a few things the Spirit clearly desires. Don't worry if you don't feel instantly passionate about all of them, or if your desire ebbs and flows. That's normal; even Paul had his moments. But if we have something of a *taste* for these things, and that desire has increased over time, it shows us the Spirit is at work in us.

> **1. The Spirit desires that Jesus is glorified.** This is his number one goal. "He will glorify me ..." says Jesus (John 16:14).
>
> **2. The Spirit desires that sin in our lives is dealt with.** It's the Spirit's job to convict us (John 16:8 NKJV).
>
> **3. The Spirit desires that people are loved and cared for.** Paul sandwiches his two chapters on spiritual gifts around 1 Corinthians 13, which describes the importance of love. The fruit of the Spirit, listed in Galatians 5:22, has love at the head of the list.

4. The Spirit desires that others come to know Jesus. The Spirit is sent to testify about Jesus (John 15:26) and is given to empower us to witness (Acts 1:8). He also gives us courage and boldness to risk all for Christ (Acts 4:31).

If you have something of a desire for these things, and you have noticed that desire increasing over time, this is a result of the Spirit's work in your life.

At another point on our trip to Israel we visited the Dead Sea. It has ten times the normal amount of salt in it and consequently everything floats and there are no fish.

As we approached, Andy noticed that Mike was incredibly reluctant to get in the water. He made excuses about not having the right swimwear and dragged his heels all the way to the beach. Eventually he admitted he was terrified he would be the only person ever to get into the Dead Sea and sink! Andy tried to explain that it was scientifically impossible for anyone to sink, but he didn't quite believe it until he tested it out for himself.

Some of us live with a quiet fear that we are the only Christians who don't have the Spirit inside us. We're the ones who will sink. If that's you, be at peace. Put simply, you want to follow Jesus, don't you? That's the result of God's Spirit inside you.

EXPERIENCING MORE

Examining our hearts reassures us of the Spirit's presence but it should also cause us to question what we are missing. Many of us still struggle with sins, feel distant from God, feel defeated in life or lack courage to witness. If we told you the spirit of Lionel Messi had come to live inside of you, you would be right to expect a dramatic increase in your football skills. If the Spirit of God is inside us, shouldn't we expect to be different?

Whilst all Christians have the Holy Spirit, there is more to experience. We use the word *experience* deliberately. Whenever the Spirit is poured out in the book of Acts it is obvious. People don't logically infer that they have the Spirit; they *know* they have received the Spirit and they can clearly see the effects. These effects include those mentioned above, but they also include: speaking in tongues (2:4; 10:46; 19:6), praising the mighty works of God (2:11; 10:46), prophesying (19:6), being given extraordinary boldness and power to witness (1:8; 6:10; 9:17, 22), obedience to God (5:32), and the working of miracles, signs and wonders (6:8; 13:9–11).

People sometimes ask whether we receive all of this at conversion, or in a subsequent outpouring of the Spirit. Some Christians argue that they received everything at conversion, they have "every spiritual blessing in Christ" (Eph. 1:3). Whilst we agree with the point of our having everything in Christ, we love the response of preacher Martyn Lloyd-Jones to those who claim they have it all: "Got it all? Well, if you have 'got it all' I simply ask, in the name of God, why are you as you are? If you have got it all, why are you so unlike the New Testament Christians? Got it all! Got it at your conversion! Well, where is it, I ask?"[1]

Others argue for a "second blessing" experience. You can come to Christ and then later be baptised in the Holy Spirit in a once-and-for-all type way. A friend of ours was once asked whether he believed in the "second blessing". He replied, "Yes, it happens between the first blessing and the third blessing!" He's right. We receive everything in Christ but we can also be filled with the Holy Spirit—not just once, but many times as we follow God.

GO ON BEING FILLED

The Holy Spirit repeatedly filled the first disciples. They received the Spirit when Jesus breathed on them (John 20:21–22) but Jesus also told them to wait in Jerusalem for the Spirit (Acts 1:4–5). On the day of Pentecost the Holy Spirit was poured out with incredible power, the disciples saw tongues of fire rest on their heads, spoke in languages they didn't know and saw three thousand people converted (Acts 2:1–12, 41). Even after the amazing experience of Pentecost the disciples continued to be filled with the Spirit. In Acts 4 they gathered to pray: "After they prayed, the place where they were meeting was shaken. And they were all filled with the Holy Spirit and spoke the word of God boldly" (v. 31).

In his letter to the Ephesians, Paul writes, "Do not get drunk on wine, which leads to debauchery. Instead, be filled with the Spirit" (Eph. 5:18). The meaning of the verse is *"Go on being filled* with the Spirit." Our lives can be like broken flasks that "leak". No matter how powerful an encounter we have with the Spirit, we will always need to go on being filled. We will face new difficulties, be called on new adventures, and be invited deeper into God. We have the Spirit, but we can know more of him.

HOW DO I RECEIVE MORE OF THE HOLY SPIRIT?

Receiving more of God's Spirit is something God offers to every one of us. How we go about it can be summarised in three simple steps: accept, ask and trust.

In Luke 11:9–13 Jesus clearly teaches how we receive the Holy Spirit:

> So I say to you: Ask and it will be given to you; seek and you will find; knock and the door will be opened to you. For everyone who asks receives; the one who seeks finds; and to the one who knocks, the door will be opened.
>
> Which of you fathers, if your son asks for a fish, will give him a snake instead? Or if he asks for an egg, will give him a scorpion? If you then, though you are evil, know how to give good gifts to your children, how much more will your Father in heaven give the Holy Spirit to those who ask him!

ACCEPT THE GIFT

First, the Holy Spirit is described as a "gift". There's nothing we do to earn a "gift". On your friend's birthday you don't give her some perfume and say, "That'll be fifty pounds. PayPal's easiest." You give her something and expect her to do nothing but receive.

This is the first thing to understand about the Holy Spirit: he is a free gift to us.

This means the outpouring of the Holy Spirit has no relation to our qualities and achievements. When it comes to a question of "merit" and being "worthy enough", the only person whose merits matter is Jesus. This is what the cross means to us. It brings us two undeserved gifts: the forgiveness of sins and the gift of the Spirit. In the Old Testament the Spirit was given to a few individuals; prophets, priests and kings. The New Testament sees a radical new outpouring, and it's the cross that makes this possible. There can be no Pentecost without Calvary; the Spirit comes from the cross.

In John 7 we read that Jesus stood up in Jerusalem and shouted, "Let anyone who is thirsty come to me and drink. Whoever believes in me, as Scripture has said, rivers of living water will flow from within them." John explains that Jesus is talking about the Holy Spirit, who "had not been given, since Jesus had not yet been glorified." (vv. 37–39). Jesus needs to be glorified—and by that we mean crucified, resurrected and ascended—in order for the Spirit to be poured out. This is why Jesus stresses to his disciples that he has to leave them, "Unless I go away, the Advocate will not come to you; but if I go, I will send him to you" (16:7).

As he was dying, Jesus said, "'It is finished.' With that, he bowed his head and gave up his spirit" (19:30). The original Greek here is ambiguous and John is known for having a fondness of double meaning. It could mean Jesus "gave up the ghost", as in, he died, but it could also be translated, "He handed over the Spirit."[2] At the very moment of death Jesus was giving over the Holy Spirit. The next thing we read is that a solider pierced Jesus's side, "bringing a sudden flow of blood and water" (v. 34). This would be typical of someone who had been killed through crucifixion but it was also symbolic. The blood of Jesus symbolises the forgiveness of sins, and the water is symbolic of the Spirit being poured out. Jesus promised that from *within us* rivers of living water would well up, but that's possible because *from him* water was poured out on the cross.

Of all the places the Spirit could have been poured out on the day of Pentecost God chose the upper room where Jesus had celebrated the Passover with the disciples. The last significant thing that had happened in that place was them eating a meal that symbolised the forgiveness of sins through the shedding of blood. The forgiveness of our sins and the giving of the Spirit go hand in hand. That is why on the day of Pentecost when Peter was preaching he said, "Repent and be baptised, every one of you, in the name of Jesus Christ for the forgiveness of your sins. And you will receive the gift of the Holy Spirit" (Acts 2:38).

So, what does this mean? We did nothing to earn our forgiveness. It was simply a case of accepting what Jesus has done for us. We receive the Spirit on exactly the same grounds. Not by doing anything, but by accepting what has been done for us.

Andy

Suppose I were to take Mike to Topman to sort out his wardrobe. I buy him two shirts—tasteful, stylish and nothing like the tat he normally wears. I pay for both shirts but Mike carelessly leaves one of them in the shop. When Mike arrives home and discovers the shirt is missing what would he do? He'd go straight back to the shop and get the shirt, but he wouldn't think for a second he'd have to pay for it. He'd explain that the shirts were a gift, remind the guy on the till they were paid for in full by me and he'd happily walk out into a more fashionable future. Wouldn't we all do the same in those circumstances?

————————

We are in those circumstances. The cross entitles us to the forgiveness of sins, and to the gift of the Spirit. Some of us have forgotten to accept the gift of the Spirit. All we need to do is recognise that he is a gift we are entitled to, explain to the Father we would like to receive him, and accept him. If you are unsure what accepting him looks like in practice, let's move on to step two: asking.

ASK FOR THE GIFT

As we saw in John 7:37, Jesus promised the Holy Spirit to anyone who is thirsty. In Luke 11 he tells us to "ask, seek and knock". We don't charge people for gifts but we do want the satisfaction that comes from giving someone something they really want. God wants to give a gift that we *eagerly desire*.

Sometimes this desire for the Spirit can come from an awareness of our own need. We can realise our own spiritual brokenness, or sorrow, or inability to change. Other times it can come from discovering in the Bible what the Spirit does in our lives. David Watson once said, "It is only the Holy Spirit who can quench the deepest thirst of the human heart, because it is only the Holy Spirit who can show us the beauty of Jesus and fill us with the love of God. Indeed, when we have drunk this glorious living water, it will spoil our thirst for everything else."[3] Romans 5:5 tells us, "God's love has been poured out into our hearts through the Holy Spirit, who has been given to us." It is God's Spirit who makes our "head" understanding of God's love a reality in our hearts.

Martyn Lloyd-Jones talked about what it's like to be filled with the Spirit:

> Let us realise then the profound character of the experience. This is not something light and superficial and ordinary; it is not something of which you can say, "Don't worry about your feelings." Worry about your feelings? You will have such a depth of feeling that for a moment you may well imagine you have never "felt" anything in your life before. It is the profoundest experience a man can ever know.[4]

Mike

I became a Christian two months before my sixteenth birthday. Straightaway I had a desperate longing to be filled with God's love, presence and power. I heard that it was possible to be filled with the Holy Spirit and I began to seek that. I asked God to fill me with his Spirit for about six months but nothing seemed to happen. I didn't know that I already had the Holy Spirit (because you can't be a Christian without the Spirit); all I knew was there was something more than I was experiencing. I asked an older couple in my church to pray for me. They invited me round to their house and prayed for the Holy Spirit to fill me. We sat waiting. And waiting. They prayed silently and, for a long time, absolutely nothing happened.

Then suddenly I was overwhelmed by the sense of God's love. I began to laugh and yet at the same time wanted to cry. I had no idea at that point that laughter could be an outward sign of God's presence, it was just the overflow of an incredible sense of joy. It was as though I could feel God's presence as a physical weight inside me. I both felt God's love in my heart and knew it in my mind in a completely new way. I realised the truth that he loves me because he loves me because he loves me.

For weeks afterwards it was as if I was walking on air. There was a sense of the nearness of God and I went around saying, "God's inside me, God's inside me!" I remember sitting on my bed day after day repeating, "You love me, Jesus. You love me. God, you're my father. You love me." I didn't get tired of it. When I read the book of Acts I read about a bunch of people who were immersed in God's love. That is what happened to me. It was dramatic. It was wonderful. And I can honestly say it was life changing. The Bible came alive in a new way. Prayer moved from being a routine to relationship. Worship was an exciting adventure. It was all about being immersed in the presence of his love.

———————

There is no secret formula to asking for the Spirit. It is simply a case of praying. We don't need to use special words, just be real and honest with God. If there are two more things to note they are:

REPENTANCE

Often we've noticed that there's a connection between repentance and being filled with the Spirit. Just last summer at one of our events there was a meeting where we gave an invitation to repent. Lots of people came forward in tears to make things right with God. It was no surprise to us that the Holy Spirit met them, nor that that evening there was an incredible outpouring of joy. Peter preached on the day of Pentecost, "Repent… And you will receive the gift of the Holy Spirit" (Acts 2:38). To repent means to "turn around". It is more than saying sorry. It is to identify the areas in our lives that are displeasing to God and seek to change. This is not to say we earn the Holy Spirit; he is a free gift from God. It is showing God we mean business and we want to have more of him in our lives.

PERSISTENCE

We aren't ordering a McDonald's or downloading an app. We're not buying a new gadget. We are seeking a relationship with—an encounter with—the living God. Jesus's teaching about asking, seeking and knocking comes in the context of a parable (Luke 11:5–8). In the parable a man had a late night visitor but didn't have any food for him. He popped round to his neighbour's and banged on the door demanding bread. His neighbour told him to clear off, but the guy just banged and yelled louder. Eventually the neighbour couldn't stand it and said that because of his "shameless audacity" he would get up and give the guy the bread he needed. We don't need to be timid when we approach God and we don't need to come up with clever words that will persuade him, we just have to unashamedly ask for as much of the Spirit as we want. And then keep asking.

Sometimes the Spirit may well fill you when you're not asking (he goes where he chooses!), but if you are looking for more of him it's important to be intentional about it.

TRUST THE GIVER

More often than not we have the gift of the Holy Spirit already, it is bought and fully paid for, but it needs to be unwrapped. We can be hindered by two obstacles that can stop us receiving the Spirit: fear of surrendering to God and unbelief that he wants to give us his Spirit.

SURRENDERING

For various reasons we can be afraid to truly trust and open ourselves up to God. We have to trust God to allow him to fill us with his Spirit, because to receive the Spirit we must relinquish control. We have to surrender.

In a remote area of China some Bible translators got stuck when they realised the language had no words for "Holy Spirit". After a lot of thought they decided that the best description in the language was "resident boss". So for a while in an area of China the Trinity was described as the Father, the Son and the Resident Boss! What a great name!

The Spirit comes to take control of our lives and he comes to *lead us* (Rom. 8:14; Gal. 5:18). The Spirit is described by Jesus as a wind that blows where it wills; we don't know where it comes from or where it is going (John 3:8). We cannot catch, domesticate or control the Spirit. Often when we think of receiving more of the Spirit we think we are getting more of some sort of power or force that we can then use for our own purposes. That is not what is happening at all! It's not that we are getting more of the Spirit so that we can use him for our will; he is getting more of us *so he can use us for his will.*

In case we are afraid to surrender, Jesus is careful to reassure us, "Which of you fathers, if your son asks for a fish, will give him a snake instead? Or if he asks for an egg, will give him a scorpion?" (Luke 11:11–12). There is no sting in the tail when God gives a gift. To surrender control to him is to surrender to a God who has selflessly and freely laid down his life for us. He is trustworthy.

Andy

For me, receiving the Holy Spirit was a gradual process. I grew up in a Christian family but for a long time faith didn't seem relevant to me. When I was about 16 or 17 I noticed my behaviour was starting to change, and that was because I'd slowly decided to follow Jesus. I was one of those people C.S. Lewis talks about when he says it's like they're on a train travelling from one country to another but they're asleep during the moment they cross the border, waking to find themselves in a whole new place.

That summer a friend dragged me along to a Christian camp. On the first night Mike was speaking and at the end he invited the Holy Spirit to minister to people. I'd never seen anything like it and yet at the same time it seemed reasonable to me that God would move in power.

Meeting Mike at that festival led me to become his intern a few years later, before I went to study theology. When I was at university, Mike invited me to lead alongside him at the Soul Survivor summer events during my holidays each year, but I spent the whole time in a state of high tension. I couldn't relax. At first I thought it was just a normal pressure that everyone was probably feeling and then I realised what the problem was: I was petrified of being out of control and had a huge fear of failure. I equated success with love and in order to succeed I thought I needed to be in control.

One year when I was particularly struggling with this Mike invited me to go to a conference where he was speaking between Soul Survivor events. I remember one afternoon there when I was feeling so weary with this battle. I wanted to be obedient to God and surrender to him and yet at the same time I wanted to be in control myself. The struggle was killing me and I believed I was failing God and therefore found it hard to receive his love and affirmation.

At one of the evening meetings I went forward for prayer to receive the Holy Spirit, saying, "Come on then, God, you need to fill me with your power." It was like getting the Holy Spirit was next on my list of things to do. Nothing happened. I stood there getting more and more frustrated but felt nothing. One of the team came over and said he saw a picture of me being like a stone in a river. The water was flowing over me and around me but not going into me and that's exactly how I felt.

The next day I went down to the beach for a walk, trying to get my frustration out as I threw pebbles into the sea, saying to God, "I want to surrender to you; I want to give you everything but it is so flipping hard." I bumped into the same team member and he could see I was upset, and offered to pray with me that I would be filled with the Holy Spirit. He said something that I've never forgotten, "Andy, your problem is not that God's going to let you go, it's that *you* won't let you go." He suggested we both pray in tongues and after a while I began to laugh. I thought it was just at this strange situation I'd found myself in, but I also felt like something had been released. Afterwards I walked back into the meeting and found myself throwing my hands in the air and jumping up and down as I worshipped the Lord; a far cry from my usual control and restraint.

For the next week I found everything hilarious, I had a new joy and a new lightness that still makes me smile when I look back at it. I've often seen God fill people with joy during worship and ministry times and that was what God had done for me—it just happened that rather than it being in a meeting, the joy overflowed from me during the following week.

EXPECTING

As well as fear, Jesus anticipated another stumbling block to our receiving the Spirit: unbelief. Maybe even as you're reading this chapter you're thinking, "This won't happen to me." In order to press home his point Jesus said the same thing in six different ways, "Ask and it will be given to you; seek and you will find; knock and the door will be opened to you. For everyone who asks receives; the one who seeks finds; and to the one who knocks, the door will be opened" (Luke 11:9–10).

This *will* happen.

We once heard someone talking about playing a game of hide and seek with his little niece, Alice. "Okay, uncle," Alice said, "These are the rules—you close your eyes and count to ten, I'm going to go and hide behind the kitchen door."

"What? Are you sure?"

"Yes, you close your eyes, count to ten, and then I'm going to hide behind the kitchen door."

Our friend counted to ten whilst Alice went and hid. Then he started "looking" for her ...

"Where's Alice, is she under the kitchen table?" (Squeals of laughter from behind the kitchen door.)

"Where's Alice, is she hiding in the cupboard?" (Squeals of laughter from behind the kitchen door.)

"Where's Alice, is she behind the kitchen door?!" Alice collapses in fits of giggles as her uncle finds her.

"Okay, uncle, let's play again. This time the rules are: you close your eyes and count to ten, I'm going to go and hide under mummy and daddy's bed ..."

In one sense God is a lot like Alice: he has told us to seek him but he has clarified the rules in advance. God wants to be found! He makes it so clear to us: "You will seek me and find me when you seek me with all your heart. I *will* be found by you" (Jer. 29:13–14).

Don't worry about seeking a particular type of experience—the two of us have had very different encounters with God and when we chat to friends about how they have met with him, the experiences are different again. We seek God's presence, not an experience. The main things to remember are: you have the Spirit living inside of you, and we can all have more of the Spirit. Our hope is that this chapter would be a springboard for you as you look to be filled with the Spirit. There is no high bar; this is part of the normal Christian life. We can all confidently and joyously expect more of God's Spirit in our lives. He is a gift the Father is willing to give to us: "How much more will your Father in heaven give the Holy Spirit to those who ask him!" (Luke 11:13).

3

GOD'S POWER, OUR WEAKNESS

*My grace is sufficient for you, for my power
is made perfect in weakness.*

2 Corinthians 12:9

Anyone who spends much time going to big Christian rallies or watching lots of Christian TV programmes can begin to think that God only uses some seemingly "anointed" men and women of God. People who preach brilliant sermons, look like models, wear expensive clothes and have every hair perfectly in place. The two of us used to think that. That is until God started using us.

Neither of us is the perfect shape. One of us is as round as he is tall. One of us is challenged when it comes to fashion (we disagree as to which one that is). And neither of us has ever felt we have given the perfect talk or led the perfect ministry time. In fact, if we're honest, we are still much more conscious of our failures than we are of our successes. We could spend the rest of this book telling you about all our failures. Perhaps one story will be sufficient ...

EVERYDAY SUPERNATURAL FOR ORDINARY PEOPLE

A little while ago, having heard many stories of folk having words for strangers in the street and those strangers being healed, delivered and coming to Jesus, we decided that we would have a go. As God's men of intrepid faith and power, we went into the centre of Watford and sat on a bench at the entrance to the shopping centre. We asked God to speak to us about who we should approach. We heard nothing. We asked again. Still nothing.

Andy

After a while I thought I had a word for an elderly gentleman who was standing by a shop window. I told Mike I was going in. He responded, "I'm covering you in prayer, brother." I approached the elderly gentleman and for a few moments stood uncomfortably next to him. When I plucked up the courage, I managed to say, "It's a very nice shop window." The elderly gentleman looked at me and shuffled a few feet away. I looked back at Mike for encouragement. (He says I was like a dog looking back at its owner for affirmation. I dispute that.) Mike gave the thumbs up, so I made a second attempt. "Do you come here often?" I asked weakly. The elderly gentleman looked at me, said, "Get lost!" (using some slightly more colourful language) and stormed away. I returned to base, tail between my legs.

Mike

After Andy's attempt, I had a sense I should look for a lady in a green coat who would have a problem in her left leg. I went on a tour of the shopping centre and after a considerable amount of time found a lady wearing a green coat in Primark. My approach could have been better. "I'm really not weird," I began, "But could I pray for your left leg?" I had hoped to have a better story than Andy but no, she too told me to get lost.

———————

There you have it. There was no happy ending. We went home with a sense of failure and humiliation. "Let's never tell anyone about this," we said to one another. As you can see, we have changed our minds.

We have become convinced that God wants to use ordinary, broken, sinful, weak, foolish people, just like us and just like you, to advance his kingdom. There is a verse that summarises this. We love it so much we even wondered about whether it should be the title of this book. It's found in 2 Corinthians 12:9. The Lord said to Paul, "My grace is sufficient for you, for my power is made perfect in weakness." Elsewhere Paul talks about how God chose the weak things of this world to shame the strong and the foolish things of this world to shame the wise. Why? Because God's longing is that we rely on him and not on ourselves (1 Cor. 1:27–29). On his wisdom, not our understanding. It's about his power in our weakness. That way all the glory goes to him.

THE WORST OF THE WORST

In New Testament times, when rabbis chose disciples they would go to the rabbinical schools and choose the best of the best. One of the questions they would ask themselves was, "Could this man do greater things than me?"

When Rabbi Jesus chose his disciples, it appears that he went for the worst of the worst. Think about them: Whenever Peter opened his mouth he put his foot in it. James and John were nicknamed "Sons of Thunder", not because they had digestive problems, but almost certainly because they were bad tempered. We're told in the gospels that they were ambitious. When Jesus had just been telling them about how he was going to die on the cross, James and John said, "Could you do us a favour? After you've done all your suffering could we sit at your right and left and be really important people?" Jesus wasn't impressed (Mark 10:35–40).

They were also competitive. As Peter and John ran to the tomb when they heard that Jesus had risen from the dead, John couldn't resist telling us that he was a faster runner than Peter (John 20:3–4). (Note: If you read the end of his book John tells us that there are many great stories he's left out—but he still thought it was important to let us know who was quickest over 100 metres ...)

They were vengeful and violent. When some Samaritan villagers didn't invite them in for a cup of tea, they suggested to Jesus that they should call down fire from heaven and have them burnt up (Luke 9:54). Jesus must have wondered whether they would ever understand.

One of the other disciples, Simon, was a Zealot. In other words, he was trying to violently overthrow the occupying Roman army.

Today he could well be labelled a terrorist. Matthew collected taxes from his own people on behalf of the occupying Roman power and was regarded as a traitor to Israel. Thomas was every pastor's worst nightmare. He was negative, wouldn't believe anything anyone said and always seemed to see the cup as half-empty. Yet Jesus *chose them*. He loved them. He was committed to them. For three years they misunderstood him and had wrong motives but Jesus didn't give up on them. In the end his love changed them and they changed the world.

If we want to look at some other characters in the Bible, think about this: Noah was a drunk, Abraham was too old, Isaac was a daydreamer, Jacob was a liar, Leah was ugly, Joseph was abused, Moses had a stutter, Gideon was afraid, Samson was a flirt, Rahab was a prostitute, Jeremiah was too young, David was an adulterer and a murderer, Elijah was suicidal, Isaiah preached naked, Jonah ran from God, Job went bankrupt, Peter denied Jesus (three times!), the disciples fell asleep whilst they were praying, the Samaritan woman was divorced (and quite possibly a sex addict), Zacchaeus was too small, Paul murdered Christians, Timothy probably had an ulcer and Lazarus was dead! If God can use a dead man he can use us.

If it's true that God's "power is made perfect in weakness" that has to mean God's power is not made perfect in our strength. Why? Because when we know *our* weakness we trust in *his* strength. That's why God delights to use people who know they are weak. So you don't need to wait until you are sorted, whole, mature and know your Bible back to front before God can use you. God can use you now. And he'll sort you, heal you and make you whole on the way.

HOW IT *REALLY* WORKS

If you came to one of our Soul Survivor events and looked at us on the stage, you might be tempted to think, *My, they seem so in control, so suave, so elegant, so sophisticated.* We need to tell you the truth: it's all an act. The fact is we both always feel weak when we step out.

Mike

On the second night of Soul Survivor B last year about two hundred young people gave their lives to Jesus. We were thrilled! The following night I was about to speak on the gift of prophecy. At the end of the worship I strode purposefully to the lectern. There was a short dramatic pause. Then I looked at the assembled nine thousand and said, "I think there is someone here called Sam. You're not a Christian and you said to your friend this morning, 'If they make an invitation for people to give their lives to Jesus tonight I think I might go forward.' Well, Sam, now is your time, where are you? Come forward, Jesus wants to meet you."

There was a long pause. But it didn't worry me; I just looked around confidently for Sam to appear. A lad got up. People around began to clap. He walked ten paces and sat down again. I was unperturbed; I knew God had spoken. After what seemed like an age a young man slowly walked forward. And when he came to the edge of the stage I asked, "Are you Sam?" The young man was trembling and nodded his head. There in front of nine thousand people Sam gave his life to the Lord. There followed a standing ovation for this young man as he walked back to his friend and the two of them were seen weeping together.

The next day others in the youth group told us that Sam had indeed been far away from God all year. He had told his friend in the morning that he might give his life to Jesus that night if the invitation was given. This story is absolutely true. I have told it, however, how I would have loved it to have happened. This is the truth:

Towards the end of the worship, a thought came into my head: *There's someone here called Sam who said to his friend if the invitation is given he'll become a Christian.* My initial reaction was, *We did a call for salvation last night; we can't do another one. And anyway it doesn't fit in with the talk on prophecy.* And then I thought, *Okay, I'll do the talk and then I'll quickly say it as a tag-on at the end.* And then the thought came into my head, *No, Mike, I want you to do it now.* I objected strongly. *What if it's me?* I thought, *What if there's no Sam? What if there is a Sam and he doesn't come forward? If I say it now, and then no one comes, I've then got to give a talk on the gift of prophecy. I will have lost all credibility! They will wonder why they should listen to a talk on the gift of prophecy from someone who is a false prophet.*

I decided I would try to do the talk instead. I tried to begin but I couldn't get my thoughts in order. And I sensed the Lord saying to me, "Is your credibility the most important thing here?" I knew that if I didn't go for it I would regret it for days. Even as I spoke the words, my mind was saying, *You idiot.* As we waited, I was already planning what I would do if Sam didn't respond. I was desperately trying to think of another talk I could give so that the false prophet didn't humiliate himself.

No one responded. I was in agony. I said to myself, *Why did you have to say this in front of nine thousand young people? Of course no one is going to come forward!* When the first guy got up and began to walk

I thought, *Thank goodness.* And then when he sat down I wanted the ground to swallow me up. I started making bargains with God: *Please get me out of this, I'll do whatever you want, I'll even go as a missionary to Wales if I have to.*

When Sam started to walk forward I was convinced that he was just heading back to his place and would sit down at any moment. When he got near the stage and said he wanted to give his life to Jesus, I nearly passed out. Not once did I feel like God's man of faith and power. Instead, I "despaired of life itself" (2 Cor. 1:8).

––––––––––––

Every time God speaks through us, or God's Spirit moves when we pray, we are honestly amazed. Please believe this is how it works. If God can use an adulterer like David, a big mouth like Peter, a doubter like Thomas and morons like the two of us, then he can use you. He uses ordinary people. All we have to do is trust his power in our weakness.

One of the reasons we're writing this book is that we believe the whole ministry of Jesus is for the whole church of Jesus. If we are ever going to tell the world effectively about Jesus we have to move from a few so-called "anointed" men and women of God. We are all anointed and God wants to use all of us to bring his kingdom.

CRACKED POTS

In 2 Corinthians 4:7 Paul says, "But we have this treasure in jars of clay to show that this all-surpassing power is from God and not from us." It's a phrase that might not mean much to us now but two thousand years ago it was a familiar image. There were no banks for people to store their money in, so rich people would keep their money hidden in expensive vases. It wasn't the best strategy because thieves would break in, grab the most expensive looking items and end up unintentionally stealing the cash inside them. People started buying cheap pottery and storing their money there to keep it safe. Paul uses this image of great treasure stored in everyday jars of clay to show that God puts the riches of his Spirit in us. He puts his treasure in ordinary cracked pots.

Too often we get the treasure and the jar confused. We can read about heroes of the faith, people like John Wesley, Hudson Taylor and Mother Teresa and think that they were used because of their gifts or abilities. If we think it's about them we've totally missed the point. It's like seeing a briefcase stuffed with millions of pounds and thinking the valuable item is the briefcase! The truth is any impact their lives had wasn't because of their abilities but because of the treasure of the Spirit within them. The weaker we are, the more we lean on God for strength. The more broken we are, the more cracks there are for the Spirit to pour out through. The history of the church has never been about great men and women of God, it's always been about the great God of men and women. Because of the grace of God when we're weak we're strong. What a relief—and what a cause for hope!

Andy

I've always placed a high value on success; at school and outside of it I tried hard at everything. When I became a Christian I couldn't get my head around the idea that God would use me in my weakness.

I had become so conditioned to the idea that strength and success are what get rewarded that "God's strength in our weakness" was a totally foreign concept to me. I remember hearing Mike speak about this on more than one occasion. He would point to his own weaknesses and tell stories about what God did despite his struggles and failings. With my head I nodded along, thinking it made sense, but in my heart I wasn't convinced. If you had pressed me, I would have admitted that I thought God used people because they were gifted. I thought he looked for strong and capable people and then made a difference through them.

I'm not sure exactly what changed my mind. It was partly seeing the people God used in the Bible. It was also spending time with Mike and others who I saw God using. As I hung around with them I began to see that the stories they told weren't for effect. They really were weak! They really did feel low, make mistakes, and find life a struggle at times. The difference between them and me was they didn't let that disqualify them. They kept going, trusting God to work despite the weakness. I also began to notice that people who—like myself—depended on themselves, tended to fill life with their own ideas, strategies and strengths, and leave very little room for God's power.

As someone who can be a success-orientated-control-freak I have always struggled to let go. But I have found over the years that the times when I step out, the times when I really am genuinely dependent on God, are the times he does the most. I did a seminar a couple of years ago at Soul Survivor that was on receiving more of the Holy Spirit. I knew that everyone in that room was expecting me to leave space at the end of the talk to invite the Holy Spirit. All I could think was, *I'll look like such an idiot if I've preached on this and then nothing happens.* I was so tempted to close by encouraging everyone to receive prayer that night in the main meeting. I knew I shouldn't so instead I took a deep breath, asked everyone to stand and prayed for the Holy Spirit to come.

No one was more surprised than me when things went crazy! There was a huge outpouring of joy and people having obvious and powerful encounters with God, the likes of which I've rarely seen when I've led a ministry time. Inside I was thinking, *I don't believe it!* while outside I was trying to act like this is exactly what we should expect to see happen when we ask the Holy Spirit to come (which it is!).

I wasn't feeling in control, confident or convinced of what would happen before I prayed. The overwhelming feeling was one of fear and trepidation. But I gave God the opportunity to work in my weakness and I was stunned by his goodness.

The tricky thing about this is we never get to the place where we don't feel weak any more. We do get more experienced and we grow in confidence that God will show up, but this side of heaven moving in the supernatural always involves weakness.

At the same event, a day later, I did another seminar. Part way through the talk I suddenly thought the Lord was saying he wanted me to invite the Holy Spirit. I carried on speaking whilst telling the Lord that it was a bad idea. *These people have come to hear me speak, Lord,* I said to the God of the universe! I didn't change my mind; I finished the seminar and walked away. I disobeyed not because I thought my talk was more important but because I was afraid. I didn't want to step out and look stupid. To this day I can't be certain whether it was God or not; I do know that I've wondered ever since what might have happened had I gone for it.

I used to regularly wish that God's power was "made perfect in our comfort zones." Recently I've changed my mind; though I still have to battle, the joy of stepping out in total dependence, utterly reliant on God, is something that I wouldn't miss for the world. If his power is truly made perfect in my weakness, the pressure is off me, the glory belongs to him, and anything is possible.

OUR WEAKNESS, GOD'S GLORY

It's vital to understand this if we want to live everyday supernatural lives. The supernatural life isn't one where we wander around with pumped-up confidence throwing power bombs at people. If it were, only a few people could ever live it. Instead, it is a life available to anyone. All we need to do is depend on God, trusting that his power can work in our vulnerability.

Our friend Ants Watts tells a story about his little girl Hannah that illustrates how this works. Ants came home one evening, and Hannah came running up to him, saying, "Daddy, Daddy, can we build a fire?" Ants agreed, and so they gathered all the bits of wood and paper they needed and arranged them in the fireplace. Once they'd lit it, Hannah knew they needed to blow on the fire to help it catch. She knelt down, put her face near the fire and began to blow. The sound was like someone blowing a raspberry. Ants said so much dribble came out of her mouth he was sure more water went on the fire than oxygen. But after a few minutes the fire suddenly caught and began to spread. Hannah turned, beaming, to her dad and said, "I did it, Daddy! I did it!" "Well done!" he responded. "You did do it, you clever girl!"

What Hannah didn't see was that whilst she was kneeling down blowing a wet raspberry at the fire, her daddy was crouching next to her. Every time she blew Ants was taking a deep breath and blowing on the fire from behind her. She turned in delight at what she'd accomplished, not knowing that her daddy had been helping her all along.

We love what that father-daughter moment illustrates about how the everyday supernatural life works. Even the "strongest" among us will only ever achieve the equivalent of a wet raspberry. But our Father is behind us. As we step out he breathes out the wind of his Holy Spirit, and fires begin to catch. Weakness is the way. This means no lack of qualifications, no lack of gifting, no lack of fashion sense can ever get in the way of God working through us. It means that you are in!

If God *delights* to use the weak then it means he delights to use you and he delights to use us. God wants to pour his treasure into your cracked pot. He wants to use you—even when you feel weak, broken, vulnerable, fearful and confused—to bring him glory.

4

DO WHATEVER HE TELLS YOU

His mother said to the servants, "Do whatever he tells you."
John 2:5

THE IMPORTANCE OF OBEDIENCE

Jesus's first ever miracle, recounted in John 2:1–11, seems to be rescuing a wedding party. Are we the only ones who think that's strange? There is a saying that you don't get a second chance to make a first impression. This seems a very tame first miracle. Surely Jesus should have announced himself by raising someone from the dead? That would have made headlines. Or even feeding five thousand people with a little boy's picnic? He could have got a lot of sermons out of that. But turning water into Châteauneuf-du-Pape at a wedding party? It seems an anticlimax. And at first sight it would appear that he only did it to calm his mother down …

When Mary said to Jesus, "They have no more wine," Jesus's response was, "Woman, why do you involve me?" (vv. 3–4). We might expect Mary to reply, "Don't talk to your mother like that." Instead she said something to the servants which we believe is foundational to the everyday supernatural: "Do whatever he tells you" (v. 5). These words can be addressed as much to us as they were to the servants.

Often we have this attitude: "Lord, we'll do what you tell us, as long as we agree with your plan. It needs to be sensible. It needs to be realistic. And we don't want to seem fanatical or extreme." We must understand that whatever we call *that*—it is not obedience. Obedience is doing what God tells us even if it doesn't seem to make sense.

After Mary told the servants, "Do whatever he tells you," Jesus then told them to fill the stone jars with water. If we had been the servants we're fairly sure we would have objected, "Excuse us, Jesus, but didn't you listen to your mother? The problem is a wine deficiency not a water shortage." We imagine that if we said this Jesus could well have replied, "Excuse me, servants, but didn't you listen to what my mother told *you*? Just to remind you, she said, 'Do whatever he tells you.' I'm telling you to fill them up with water." The servants obeyed.

Then Jesus told them to do something that seemed even crazier: to fill a cup with water and take it to the master of ceremonies. Somewhere on the journey between the water jar and the master of ceremonies a miracle happened. Water became wine. How did it happen? The answer has to be because they did what Jesus told them. What Jesus told them didn't make sense. What might have made sense would have been him lending them his American Express and sending them down to the off-licence. We might well have obeyed him had he told us to do that! However, obedience is doing *whatever he tells us*, regardless of whether we understand. The servants must have been pretty mystified but they obeyed anyway.

It is our utter conviction that if we want to see the water of broken bodies, broken minds and broken hearts turned into the wine of whole people, we need to do whatever he tells us. It often won't make sense. It will rarely be comfortable. Yet this kind of obedience to Jesus is the practical outworking of faith and the tangible expression of love.

OBEDIENCE AND FRIENDSHIP

Andy loves his son Josiah, who at the time of writing has just celebrated his first birthday. Andy and Josiah have a great father-son relationship but they cannot at the moment be described as friends. They don't sit over breakfast discussing the political or economic situation. Andy isn't pouring his heart out to Josiah about his struggles leading a church with Mike. However, if all goes well, when Josiah reaches the age of twenty, in addition to having a father-son relationship they will also be friends.

We believe that God has many children but he doesn't have many friends and he is looking for more. In John 15:15 Jesus says, "I no longer call you servants, because a servant does not know his master's business. Instead, I have called you friends, for everything that I learned from my Father I have made known to you." Jesus says that he reveals all the family secrets to his friends. So how do we become friends of Jesus? He gives us the answer, "You are my friends if you do what I command" (John 15:14).

Obedience is the key to friendship with Jesus. He also tells us, "If you love me, keep my commands" (John 14:15). Of course human friendships don't work like that. We wouldn't advise you to say to someone, "You are my friend if you do *exactly* what I tell you." That might seem more than a little manipulative and domineering. However, our relationship with Jesus is unique. Many of us are so used to the idea of God's overwhelming love that we can overlook the fact that we are not in an equal relationship with him. He is the Lord and we are the servants. He is the king and we are his subjects. He is the general and we are his soldiers. Friendship with Jesus always involves obedience to Jesus.

STEPPING OUT OF THE BOAT

Much like the servants at the wedding, Jesus repeatedly told the disciples to do things that made no sense. On one occasion he said, "Go to the village ahead of you, and as you enter it, you will find a colt tied there, which no one has ever ridden. Untie it and bring it here. If anyone asks you, 'Why are you untying it?' say, 'The Lord needs it'" (Luke 19:30–31). Elsewhere he said, "As you enter the city, a man carrying a jar of water will meet you. Follow him to the house that he enters, and say to the owner of the house, 'The Teacher asks: Where is the guest room, where I may eat the Passover with my disciples?'" (Luke 22:10–11).

It's easy to read these stories and gloss over how strange they must have seemed. A modern equivalent would be walking into a car showroom and saying, "Give me the Ford Fiesta, the Lord needs it." Or following someone home from Sainsbury's and saying, "Where's your spare room? I'm bringing twelve of my friends round for a meal." It would have been no easier for the disciples then than it would be for us today.

In Matthew 14:22–33 there's another amazing story about Jesus. Having turned water into wine, he's now going for a stroll on some H^2O:

Immediately Jesus made the disciples get into the boat and go on ahead of him to the other side, while he dismissed the crowd. After he had dismissed them, he went up on a mountainside by himself to pray. Later that night, he was there alone, and the boat was already a considerable distance from land, buffeted by the waves because the wind was against it.

Shortly before dawn Jesus went out to them, walking on the lake. When the disciples saw him walking on the lake, they were terrified. "It's a ghost," they said, and cried out in fear.

But Jesus immediately said to them: "Take courage! It is I. Don't be afraid."

"Lord, if it's you," Peter replied, "tell me to come to you on the water."

"Come," he said.

Then Peter got down out of the boat, walked on the water and came towards Jesus. But when he saw the wind, he was afraid and, beginning to sink, cried out, "Lord, save me!"

Immediately Jesus reached out his hand and caught him. "You of little faith," he said, "why did you doubt?"

And when they climbed into the boat, the wind died down. Then those who were in the boat worshipped him, saying, "Truly you are the Son of God."

For years when reading this passage we have misread the first sentence. Matthew tells us that Jesus *made* the disciples get into the boat. In the original Greek it's a strong word. This wasn't a mild suggestion; Jesus sent them *into* the Sea of Galilee, at night, in bad weather. Sometimes Jesus deliberately sends us into storms. Why? Because it's often in the storms of life that we find greater intimacy with Jesus and can see the greatest miracles. That is exactly what happened to Peter in this story.

In the early hours of the morning the wind was strong and the waters were rough. Jesus walked to the disciples through the waves. They were terrified, thinking he was a ghost.

Sometimes in the storms of life we can get so fearful that we don't recognise Jesus when he comes to us. Jesus said to them, "Take courage! It is I. Don't be afraid" (v. 27). They heard his voice and the fear subsided. When Jesus speaks, fear goes and faith comes. Romans 10:17 says, "Faith comes from hearing the message, and the message is heard through the word about Christ." When the disciples heard Jesus speak, they recognised him. This is one reason why we need to read, know and love our Bibles. The main place Jesus speaks to us is through his book.

Peter got very excited and said, "Lord, if it's you, tell me to come to you on the water." That is always a great thing to say to Jesus: "If it's you, speak to me and I'll obey." Jesus responded with one word: "Come." Peter got out and he started walking on the water. Before long our "hero" took his eyes off Jesus and was looking at the waves. He became scared and began to sink. "Lord, save me!" he cried out.

HAND IN HAND WITH JESUS

For years we have assumed that Peter failed. In fact, we now see that he was the only one of the twelve who succeeded. We can read on to see why: "Immediately Jesus reached out his hand and caught him. 'You of little faith,' he said, 'why did you doubt?' And when they climbed into the boat, the wind died down" (Matt. 14:31–32). Many of us have read these words with our own spin:

> Peter begins to drown. He calls out, "Lord, save me," as he goes under the water. Jesus dives into the water. He does the front crawl through the waves. Jesus uses a life-saving technique he learnt at Nazareth swimming pool. He shouts at the disciples, "Quick, throw the rubber ring!" They drag a semi-unconscious Peter into the boat. Jesus then gives him mouth-to-mouth resuscitation. And then, as Peter is coughing up water, Jesus shouts at him, "YOU OF LITTLE FAITH, WHY DID YOU DOUBT?"

That is not actually what happened. Matthew tells us that as Peter started to sink, Jesus reached out his hand and caught him. Jesus held his hand and the clear implication of the passage is that *they walked back to the boat, hand in hand, on the water.* Can you imagine the intimacy Peter must have felt walking through huge waves holding hands with Jesus?

If Jesus was holding Peter's hand it is unlikely he was also shouting angrily into his ear. We suspect that the tone might have been a little more like this, "Oh, Pete, you twit! Why didn't you trust me? Did you really think I'd let you drown?" Far from this being a story about Peter's failure, we suspect that the great apostle dined out on this tale for the rest of his life. He was obedient when Jesus told him to get out of the boat. He got to be involved in a miracle and walk hand in hand with Jesus. When we obey and get out of the boat of our safety and security it can feel scary. Sometimes we can feel like we're drowning but Jesus holds our hand and walks with us. (Then we often talk about it afterwards as if we helped Jesus along!) So far, on the other side of a few storms we've experienced, we can say we wouldn't have missed any of the adventures for the world.

We have lost count of the number of times before our summer events begin where we have found ourselves pacing up and down, feeling out of our depth, and saying something like, "Lord, save us, it feels like we're drowning." Inevitably a few weeks later we are rejoicing and telling stories of his kindness, his power and his love. Each time we have known the intimacy of tightly holding his hand and seeing miracles happen.

DOING WHATEVER HE TELLS US

This works out in different ways for all of us but it generally involves the ingredients of Peter's story. We have to step out. We often feel frightened and as if we are drowning but there we discover intimacy with Jesus. And afterwards, like the disciples, we end up worshipping him, full of awe at who Jesus is.

Mike

About four years ago I sensed God challenging me to step out of my comfort zone and to choose to obey him when I didn't completely understand what he was telling me to do. For me, the main practical outworking has been in church and conference meetings, because that's where my job calls me to spend a lot of time.

On one occasion at our Momentum event for twenties and thirties I felt God speak to me during the worship. I was shocked at what came into my head. "There is someone here who is having an affair with a pastor in their church." Everything in me recoiled at that word. "There is no way I'm saying that," I said to myself. "It goes against all our rules. It's a negative word. And anyway, how am I supposed to invite that person to come forward in front of six thousand people?" I was on my way to overruling God when I remembered my promise. Also the Lord said to me, "It's not my judgment, Mike. It's my mercy." I wanted to weep as for a moment he opened a window in my heart to sense something of his compassion for this person.

My responsibility was to be obedient in giving the word but also to work out how to do it in a way that was pastorally sensitive. I gave the message and then said, "If that's you, please come and see my friend Ali at any time during the meeting or go to one of our counsellors tomorrow. We would love to pray for you that God would heal you and set you free." At the end of the meeting a young lady came up to Ali in floods of tears. She said she had been having an affair with the youth pastor in her church who was married with three children and she didn't know how to stop. As she was driving to Momentum she said to God, "I'm too ashamed to tell anyone about this. Lord, if you want this relationship to end, you're going to have to tell someone on the stage about it because I can't tell anyone."

Members of our team prayed for her and she repented and stopped the relationship and went through a process of healing and restoration. When I heard about this, I was astounded. I came within an inch of not saying anything. If I had kept my mouth shut she would have missed the blessing. On the other hand, if I had made a mistake and no one had responded to that word, nobody would have died. How kind is God? I saw him at work, but it only happened as I got out of the boat, began to sink, cried out, "Lord, help me", and had the joy of walking on the water holding his hand.

GOD'S LOVE LANGUAGE

If you have been a Christian for more than three minutes, you've probably heard of the book *The 5 Love Languages* by Gary Chapman. The theory is that we all have one of five particular ways of giving and receiving love, whether it's gifts, quality time, words of affirmation, physical touch or acts of service. There are variations on the theme. There's a book called *The 5 Love Languages of Children*, one for teenagers and another called *The 5 Love Languages Singles Edition*. We're fairly sure that at some stage someone will bring out *The 5 Love Languages for Left-Handed People*. Mike recently made a discovery that Andy always suspected: he has a sixth love language—food. Say something nice to Mike and it seems to mean nothing to him. Buy him a kebab and he is yours for life.

Much more importantly, we have discovered that God has a love language. As you will have guessed from reading this chapter, it is obedience. To quote John 14:15 again, Jesus says, "If you love me, keep my commands." Jesus is not talking as an insecure boyfriend or girlfriend would, rather he's making a statement of fact. God loves obedience because it is the ultimate expression of friendship with him. Obedience is the ultimate act of worship. It is also an act of faith because it's an act of trusting love. In 1 Samuel 15:22 we read, "To obey is better than sacrifice." If we want to show God we love him, one act of obedience is better than a hundred sacrifices he hasn't asked for.

ANOINTING AND OBEDIENCE

You've probably heard many people talk of how "anointed" someone is as an evangelist or in praying for healing. This is another way of saying they are effective at it. Jesus was called the "anointed one" which is translated "Messiah" in Hebrew and "Christ" in Greek. So to be anointed is to have the power and presence of Jesus in us. We've become increasingly convinced that anointing and obedience are linked. The most "anointed" people we know are, coincidentally, the most obedient in the area where they seem anointed.

Our friend J.John is a great evangelist. Whenever he preaches the gospel many people respond. Mike has been puzzled by this as he and J.John often share talks and illustrations. (J.John writes the talks and illustrations and Mike likes to think that he improves on them.) Mike doesn't see anything like the number of people becoming Christians when he gives essentially the same talk that J.John would give. One day when Mike and John went out for lunch together Mike realised why.

The waitress came over to them with the menu and John began to chat with her. "How are you?" he asked. "How long have you worked here?" Mike was very hungry and began to groan. When John began to ask her what she would like to do with her life, Mike became desperate. At one point he wanted to shout, "Let her go to hell, I haven't had my lunch yet!" By the end of the meal John had given her a copy of one of the gospels and she had promised to read it. They'd agreed he would return in a week so they could discuss what she had read. One of the reasons J.John is more "anointed" as an evangelist than Mike is because John is willing to tell people about Jesus *before* lunch. He doesn't wait until it's convenient, comfortable or safe. The anointing rides on obedience.

God will command all of us to step out of our boats and trust him. Expect to hear his command, "Come to me on the water." Then go, even though it seems risky and frightening. The best place to practise this obedience is in the everyday. It means being obedient even when it's mundane and no one is looking. It means obeying the commands he gives us about how we spend our time, our money and our talents. Our culture is full of invitations to self-fulfilment and self-discovery. The truth is we don't need to discover more about ourselves, we need to find more of Jesus. He himself said that anyone who would try to find his life would lose it, yet anyone who lost his life for the sake of the gospel would find it (Luke 9:24). The hope for the world is a church that lives in radical obedience to the king. This is the foundation of the everyday supernatural.

So let's take Mary's advice: "Do whatever he tells you."

5

EVERYONE GETS TO PLAY: INTRODUCING THE GIFTS

*Now about the gifts of the Spirit, brothers and
sisters, I do not want you to be uninformed."*

1 Corinthians 12:1

We have a world to win for Jesus. There is a kingdom to be built and this is not something we can do in our own strength. Jesus encouraged his disciples to wait for "power" to be his witnesses (Acts 1:8). Like the disciples, we are empowered as we are filled with the Holy Spirit and the Spirit gives us gifts that are tools to build the kingdom.

SOMEONE ELSE'S MAIL

Whenever we read one of the letters in the New Testament we are reading one half of a conversation. In the case of 1 Corinthians we are reading what Paul wrote to a church that he founded in Corinth (see Acts 18). We don't have any letters the Corinthians might have written to Paul, but by reading Paul's letter carefully we can see that he is responding both to questions they have asked him and reports he has heard about them.

In 1 Corinthians 12–14 Paul is talking about community worship and particularly dealing with the spiritual gifts. The Corinthians had been over emphasising the showier gifts and their worship ended up completely chaotic and self-centred. Paul addresses this not by telling them to stop using the gifts but by making clear what the gifts are for.

It's worth reading 1 Corinthians 12:1–11 again:

> Now about the gifts of the Spirit, brothers and sisters, I do not want you to be uninformed. You know that when you were pagans, somehow or other you were influenced and led astray to dumb idols. Therefore I want you to know that no one who is speaking by the Spirit of God says, "Jesus be cursed," and no one can say, "Jesus is Lord," except by the Holy Spirit.
>
> There are different kinds of gifts, but the same Spirit distributes them. There are different kinds of service, but the same Lord. There are different kinds of working, but in all of them and in everyone it is the same God at work.
>
> Now to each one the manifestation of the Spirit is given for the common good. To one there is given through the Spirit a message of wisdom, to another a message of knowledge by means of the same Spirit, to another faith by the same Spirit, to another gifts of healing by that one Spirit, to another miraculous

powers, to another prophecy, to another distinguishing between spirits, to another speaking in different kinds of tongues, and to still another the interpretation of tongues. All these are the work of one and the same Spirit, and he distributes them to each one, just as he determines.

GIFTS OF GRACE

Some of the Corinthians seemed to see the gifts as things to boast about; they were using them to show off. In just a few verses Paul pulls the rug out from under their feet.

First, he says, the one certain activity of the Spirit is that he leads people to Jesus: "No one can say 'Jesus is Lord,' except by the Holy Spirit" (v. 3). This means *everyone* who follows Jesus has the Spirit living inside them. People who are using spiritual gifts do not have some sort of "special access"; they aren't superior to anyone else.

Second, in verse 1 Paul uses a Greek word, *pneumatikon*, which is often translated "spiritual gifts" but simply means "spiritual things". Then in verse 4 he switches and uses *charismata* to describe the gifts, a word meaning "gifts of grace". It is the Spirit who *graciously gives* the gifts. If the gifts are freely given and aren't based on our goodness, spirituality or intelligence then we have nothing to be proud about. It is as ridiculous to boast about having the gift of prophecy as it is to boast about having blue eyes.

The gifts are not trophies to show off in a cabinet, or badges to wear but rather tools to be used. They are necessary for strengthening the church and bringing the good news of Jesus to the world.

THE TOOLKIT

There are different lists of spiritual gifts in the New Testament. The other main lists can be found in 1 Corinthians 12:28, Romans 12:6–8 and Ephesians 4:11. You may notice there's some overlap between them. The nine gifts mentioned in 1 Corinthians 12:7–10 are not meant to be exclusive; they are examples rather than a comprehensive list of the spiritual gifts. We are going to limit ourselves to the list in 1 Cor. 12:7–10 because there has been a lot of misunderstanding about these seemingly more supernatural gifts. We'll give a very brief overview of these gifts here, and in the following chapters we will go on to look at some of them in more depth.

WORD OR KNOWLEDGE GIFTS

Word of Wisdom

This is when supernatural insight is given to us for a particular issue or person when we have no idea what to do. A word of wisdom is when we operate with God–given perception or astuteness that allows us to direct people towards God's freedom and life. We see an example of this in 1 Kings 3:16–28. Two women were brought to King Solomon, both claiming a baby was their own. How could Solomon judge between them in the days before DNA testing? He ordered that the child should be cut in half and each woman given a share. The true mother then relinquished her claim rather than see the child die.

King Solomon prayed and asked God to give him supernatural wisdom and God gave him the gift. We are told in the letter of

James, "If any of you lacks wisdom, you should ask God, who gives generously to all without finding fault, and it will be given to you" (James 1:5).

Prophecy and Words of Knowledge

The gift of prophecy is God's "now" word to a group or person that strengthens, encourages and comforts them. It is a specific message that is supernaturally given. Sometimes these prophetic insights can come in the form of a talk, a message or even a song. We see this with Simeon, Zechariah and Mary at the birth of Jesus, as well as Peter on the day of Pentecost.

A word of knowledge is similar to prophecy; the distinction would probably be that a word of knowledge would involve a more specific revelation of a person's situation or condition. There are plenty of examples of both Jesus and the early church using these gifts, such as in John 4:17–29, Matthew 17:27 and Acts 9:10–15.

Discerning between Spirits

This is a supernatural revelation that gives us insight into the source or motivation underlying a person's behaviour, or a situation. Of course there is a discernment that is natural but here we are talking about a sense that comes from the Holy Spirit. An example of the gift in practice might be a scenario where, on the surface everything seems okay and there is no natural reason to be concerned, but you develop an uneasy feeling in your spirit. Sometimes when praying for people you have a sense of whether the root of the issue is physical, emotional or spiritual. Jesus was able to supernaturally recognise the good in Nathanael, and the error in Peter's rebuke (see John 1:47

and Matthew 16:23). We need to be cautious, however, that we don't baptise our judgmental attitudes as "discerning between spirits".

Tongues and Interpretation of Tongues

The gift of tongues is the supernatural ability to speak in a language that is unknown to the speaker. It can be an actual foreign language and even the language of angels (1 Cor. 13:1). Interpretation of tongues is when revelation of the meaning of a particular tongue is given to someone else so that it might be shared with the group. There are many instances of believers praying in tongues in Acts and, as we'll see, this was certainly something that was practised in Corinth. For examples in Acts check out Acts 2:4, 10:45–46 and 19:6.

POWER GIFTS

Faith

This gift looks like a particular moment where you suddenly have supernatural expectancy or trust that causes you to step out in a way you wouldn't normally. It also seems to coincide with a supernatural authority to carry out God's plans. You may have a sudden confidence that if you pray for someone they will be healed, or that you should approach a particular person in the street. It isn't something that we work up; it is given in a particular moment. We've noticed that often after the use of this gift we think, "What on earth was I doing? I can't believe I said that!" This gift will frequently operate alongside the other gifts (like healing), but we almost certainly see an example of it when Peter commanded the lame beggar to walk in Acts 3:2–7.

Gifts of Healing

This is when God uses us to supernaturally heal a disease or infirmity. Jesus healed people from all sorts of conditions, so did his followers. For just a few of many examples see Mark 1:30–34, 3:1–5, Acts 5:15–16 and 28:8–9. We'll talk much more about this in a later chapter.

Miraculous Powers

A miracle is a more unusual divine act. It often causes people to wonder, inspires awe and bears witness to God. It is where God's power operates through someone and supernaturally intervenes in the natural order of things. The line between healing and miraculous powers is blurred. In Jesus's ministry he was able not just to heal those who had fallen sick, but create where something had never existed. For example, see the stir caused by him healing a man *born* blind (John 9:1–34), or the resurrection of Lazarus (John 11:38–44; 12:9–11).

Turning water into wine, calming a storm, walking on water and feeding five thousand with a small picnic would also fall into this group! Examples of "miraculous powers" in Acts might be the casting out of demons, the striking of Elymas blind, and the raising of Tabitha from the dead (Acts 16:18, 13:11–12 and 9:40).

ARE THE GIFTS FOR ME?

The gifts of the Spirit are for every believer who wants them. Everyone gets to play! Paul is writing 1 Corinthians 12–14 to address a problem in the gathered community of believers. Their worship services were out of control. People were boasting about their gifts and acting

like "super Christians". Paul makes it clear that the Spirit gives gifts
to *everyone* and that in the gathered meeting no one person gets all
the gifts. If we want to participate in the supernatural we shouldn't
be looking to any one person but to the Spirit.

It is the case that sometimes people are so faithful in exercising
a particular gift that they develop a ministry in a particular area.
This seems to be what Paul's list in 1 Corinthians 12:27–30 is about.
It's possible for someone to use the gift of prophecy so much that
the church begins to look to them to exercise that gift. They have
developed a ministry as a prophet. The same might be true of teaching, evangelism, pastoring and so on. It doesn't follow that because
we don't have the ministry of a prophet we can't prophesy. We might
not be evangelists or pastors, but we are all meant to witness and love
each other. All of us are also *actively encouraged* to hear God speak,
pray for the sick and speak in tongues. We are all able to play, so
never rule yourself out of being able to use these gifts.

Do you want God to use you? Do you long to see God's power
flow through you to set people free? Do you want your words to
bring a revelation of Jesus into people's hearts and minds? The
Bible condemns what it calls "selfish ambition", but there is a good
ambition. And we should all be ambitious for God to use us in his
kingdom. Ask him to give you lots of "talents", and then don't bury
them, invest them. This is the one time we're allowed to be greedy.
Why? Because, "the one who prophesies speaks to people for their
strengthening, encouragement and comfort" (1 Cor. 14:3). We
assume that you, like us, want to strengthen, encourage and comfort
other people. Then seek the gift of prophecy. We could say the same
for miracles, healings, gifts of discernment and all the above.

Our purpose in the next few chapters is to help us all come to a place where we understand the gifts enough to start using them. Just to underline one last time before we go on: the gifts of the Spirit are not status symbols or rewards for spirituality. They are God's power freely given to normal, weak people so they can be effective in bringing about his kingdom in this world.

6

PRAYING IN TONGUES

I would like every one of you to speak in tongues.

1 Corinthians 14:5

On first appearance, the gift of tongues seems like the strangest of the gifts. The idea of speaking in languages we haven't learnt seems both far-fetched and bizarre. Yet is it totally biblical and many Christians, including the two of us, have found it a helpful and beneficial way to pray. We'll begin by looking at what the Bible says about tongues and move on to talk about how you can receive this gift.

THE DAY OF PENTECOST

Praying in tongues is something that is closely associated with an outpouring of the Holy Spirit. On the day of Pentecost, when the Holy Spirit came upon the first disciples, Scripture tells us that, "All of them were filled with the Holy Spirit and began to speak in other tongues as the Spirit enabled them" (Acts 2:4). Elsewhere, when Cornelius and his household were filled with the Spirit we read, "The circumcised believers who had come with Peter were astonished that the gift of the Holy Spirit had been poured out even on Gentiles. For they heard them speaking in tongues and praising God" (Acts 10:45–46). When Paul came across some believers in Ephesus who hadn't yet been baptised in the name of Jesus we're told he "placed his hands on them, the Holy Spirit came on them, and they spoke in tongues and prophesied" (Acts 19:6).

We both once thought that in order to pray in tongues we had to wait for the Holy Spirit to take over our mouths. In fact, the way it actually happens feels far more "everyday". In the same way that with prophecy we need to take a step of faith, and with praying for healing we need to lay on hands and pray, speaking in tongues isn't something that just happens to us outside of our control, it is something that we are enabled to do in cooperation with the Holy Spirit. Acts 2:4 tells us that the disciples *spoke* as the Spirit *enabled* them. The gift of tongues requires our speaking and the Spirit's enabling.

David Pytches's definition is helpful: "'Speaking in tongues' or 'praying in the Spirit' is what happens when a Christian believer allows the indwelling Spirit to guide the form of words he utters. It is not an act of divine ventriloquism, but an act of collaboration.[1]"

Some people argue that speaking in tongues is an automatic result of being filled with the Spirit, but we don't think the Bible teaches this. Not everyone who is filled with the Spirit has to speak in tongues, but it is clearly a gift of the Spirit—and it is one that Paul encourages all of us to pursue.

1 CORINTHI-TONGUES

[Author's note: Andy would like to apologise for the horrendous pun. It happened when he was out of the room.]

GETTING THE CONTEXT

As we've seen, Paul's first letter to the Corinthian church was aimed at helping them use the gifts of the Spirit better. This is particularly true of the gift of tongues.

It is generally accepted that there are three different manifestations of the gift of tongues. They have Greek names that make "Pilavachi" seem easy to spell:

> 1. **Xenoglossolalia** (drop that into your next Bible study). This is when the speaker prays in an actual foreign language. It is a language they don't know but is known by one of the hearers without any interpretation needed. This is what happened in Acts 2:4–8.
>
> 2. **Glossolalia** (the general word used for speaking in tongues). This sometimes happens in the context of public worship. Someone might call out in a tongue and neither the speaker, nor the hearer knows the language so an interpretation through the Holy Spirit is needed (see 1 Cor. 14:13).

3. **Praying in Tongues in Private** (Okay, that's not a Greek name but it's the personal/private use of glossolalia and we weren't sure what else to call it).[2]

The problem Paul is trying to address in his letter is a misuse of glossolalia. The Corinthians were getting very excited and seemingly standing up, giving long speeches in tongues one after the other. Neither they nor anyone else understood, and they didn't seem bothered about an interpretation. Paul was a passionate evangelist and he was worried about what the non-Christians would think. Imagine how bonkers a Sunday at their church must have seemed! After the third sermon in a language not even the speaker understood, the visitors would be quietly wishing they'd stayed in bed.

WHAT IS PAUL SAYING?

With this context in mind you may find it helpful to read through 1 Corinthians 14. Paul is basically telling the Corinthians to stop doing this. His reason is that spiritual gifts are primarily given to build up the church and no one is blessed by a long speech in a language that they don't understand. "Unless you speak intelligible words with your tongue, how will anyone know what you are saying? You will just be speaking into the air" (v. 9). To give a long speech without interpretation is self-indulgent, "You are giving thanks well enough, but no one else is edified" (v. 17).

He tells them, "Since you are eager for gifts of the Spirit, try to excel in those that build up the church" (v. 12). Paul is thinking particularly of prophecy as the gift that is most useful for building up others:

> Anyone who speaks in a tongue edifies themselves, but the one who prophesies edifies the church. I would like every one of you to speak in tongues, but I would rather have you prophesy. The one who prophesies is greater than the one who speaks in tongues, unless someone interprets, so that the church may be edified. (vv. 4–5)

He instructs the Corinthians to either make sure there is an interpretation or to stop speaking in tongues in this way.

This is Paul's guidance for a public meeting, but tongues are also used for personal prayer. The very same chapter of 1 Corinthians gives us all sorts of clues that Paul highly valued this. He writes, "I thank God that I speak in tongues more than any of you." Here he is referring to his personal devotional life, because he goes on to say, "But in the church I would rather speak five intelligible words …" (vv. 18–19). He is saying that in his private prayer life he speaks in tongues more than anyone, but in the church he would rather bless other people than bless himself. This was a gift that Paul wanted to be used correctly; it was a gift that he treasured.

One of the unique aspects of the gift of tongues is that it builds up, or edifies, the person who uses it. "Anyone who speaks in a tongue edifies themselves …" (v. 4). No doubt this was why Paul spoke in tongues so much. Do you want to be built up as you follow

Jesus? Then we suggest one of the things you can do is seek the gift of tongues. That's why Paul wants all of us to speak in tongues (v. 5). We agree with the apostle Paul and would love for each one of us to speak in tongues.

PRAYING IN THE SPIRIT

As Paul said, speaking in tongues is a form of prayer that builds us up (1 Cor. 14:2, 4) and we have both found the gift of tongues incredibly helpful in our prayer lives. We have also found that when we pray in tongues we are more sensitised to God and to the other gifts of the Spirit. Praying in tongues has proved such a blessing to us because it is a form of praying in the Spirit.

One of the great needs of today is that we learn to be led by the Spirit in our prayers as much as in our actions. Paul writes, "If I pray in a tongue, my spirit prays, but my mind is unfruitful. So what shall I do? I will pray with my spirit, but I will also pray with my understanding; I will sing with my spirit, but I will also sing with my understanding" (vv. 14–15).

We are all used to praying with our minds, and this is a good thing that Paul affirms. But learning to pray in the Spirit can be quite an adventure.

Did you realise that two members of the Trinity—Jesus and the Holy Spirit—are praying for us to God the Father? Jesus (our great high priest) is praying for us apart from us, at the right hand of the Father (Hebrews 7:25). He is praying for you even as you're reading this book (though we don't want to speculate exactly what he's praying!).

The Holy Spirit is also praying for us, but is not praying apart from us, but from within us. He joins with our spirit so it's a joint prayer. The gift of tongues is one great way he does that. This is why we are built up. When we pray in tongues we are praying the prayers of the Holy Spirit, with the Holy Spirit, to the Father. How amazing is that?

WORDS FOR THE SOUL

Perhaps you've been in a situation where you've loved someone so much you battle to find the words to express yourself. (For Andy it's a situation he can relate to when he's with his wife, Beth. For Mike he feels something similar whenever he meets the owner of a Mexican restaurant.) When we come to worship God we can run out of ways to tell him we love him. The gift of tongues isn't mindless; this isn't what Paul means when he says his mind is "unfruitful." But it is prayer that doesn't need our mind to find the words. When we run out of words in English the gift of tongues allows worship to pour out of our spirits in the Holy Spirit. On the day of Pentecost, the disciples burst out of the room declaring "the wonders of God" (Acts 2:11). The gift of tongues enabled them to worship and express their hearts to God.

As well as helping us praise, the gift of tongues helps us pray. Praying in the Spirit is referred to by Paul in Romans 8:26–27, "We do not know what we ought to pray for." Anyone know that feeling? He goes on, "But the Spirit himself intercedes for us through wordless groans. And he who searches our hearts knows the mind of the Spirit, because the Spirit intercedes for God's people in accordance with the will of God."

Paul is talking about more than just praying in tongues here, but praying in tongues is an essential way to depend on the Spirit when we pray. Often we come to God with our lists and we get stuck after a few minutes of praying for the same person. The Spirit can help. Sometimes when we don't know what to say, or when something serious is happening and we're too concerned about it to think clearly, it can be great to pray in tongues. The Holy Spirit always knows what to pray for, and he prays through each of us. What an incredible thought.

DRAWING NEAR

In verses 20–21 of Jude we read, "Praying in the Holy Spirit, keep yourselves in God's love."

In his book on prayer R.A. Torrey describes something we can all relate to: trying to pray and feeling as though we are just talking to air. He says,

> Shall we stop praying and wait until sometime when we feel like praying? No, when we least feel like praying, and when God is least real to us, is the time we need most to pray. What shall we do then? … Simply be quiet, and look up to God and ask God to fulfill His promise and send His Holy Spirit to lead us into His presence and the Holy Spirit will make God real to us. Then wait and expect. And He will come.[3]

It is the Spirit's job to lead us into the presence of God and to make God real to us. Praying in tongues is not the only way this happens but it is one of them.

Occasionally, the two of us do crazy things. Once we were driving from Watford to Somerset, a journey of two and a half hours, and we prayed in tongues, out loud, all the way. By the time we arrived we were ready to explode. We were laughing and were both so aware of the presence and the glory of God with us. We prayed in the Spirit for two and a half hours and we were built up, edified and fed.

While the Bible says the gift of tongues isn't the most important of the gifts, it can be a phenomenal blessing when we use it well. Often when we pray in the Spirit we are more aware not only of God's presence but his love. Which of us wouldn't want more of that?

BREAKING THROUGH

Paul encourages the church in Ephesus to "pray in the Spirit on all occasions with all kinds of prayers and requests" (Eph. 6:18). The context is one of spiritual warfare and as Jesus's followers we often face a battle to bring God's kingdom on the earth. Prayer is one of the key ways we fight that battle. Although speaking in tongues builds up the person praying, it can also have a powerful indirect effect on others. God's ability to surprise us in the way that he uses this gift never ceases to amaze us.

Mike

A few years ago we were in an evening meeting at Soul Survivor and we prayed for people to receive the gift of tongues. Every year we get visitors from different countries and this year there happened to be a youth group from Romania. The youth leader from this group didn't believe in the gift of tongues so as we invited the Holy Spirit, he got up and began to walk out. As people were beginning to pray, the rest of us in the Big Top began to speak out praise to God, either in English or in tongues. I happened to be praying over the microphone in tongues and I noticed it seemed a little different to me. I even wondered if I was subconsciously trying to make it sound better as so many people could hear me.

Afterwards a couple of young people from the Romanian group ran up to me and said that as I'd started speaking their youth leader had stopped in his tracks. He had been stunned because he recognised the language I was speaking in; apparently it was ancient Romanian. According to him I was reciting an eleventh century Romanian poem called the "Prayer for Protection". To add to that, he knew the words because the poem was one that had been tattooed on his father's back. That youth leader now believes in the gift of tongues!

———————

There have been many people who have seen all sorts of miraculous advances when they have prayed in tongues. Jackie Pullinger's story is well known. She went to Hong Kong as a young woman and found herself ministering among drug addicts and the Triad gangs. She was struggling to make any sort of impact until she began to pray in tongues. She writes about how she used the gift:

> By the clock I prayed 15 minutes a day in the language of the Spirit and still felt nothing as I asked the Spirit to help me intercede for those he wanted to reach. After about six weeks of this I began to lead people to Jesus without trying. Gangsters fell to their knees sobbing in the streets, women were healed, heroin addicts were miraculously set free. And I knew it was nothing to do with me.[4]

Jackie would say it had nothing to do with her actions, and everything to do with her praying in tongues for fifteen minutes a day.

The gift of tongues supplies words for our souls, draws us into God's love and can powerfully advance the kingdom of God. How amazing is that?

HOW TO RECEIVE THE GIFT OF TONGUES

BELIEVE

If we're going to receive the gift of tongues, it really helps to believe that God wants to give it to us. God wants all of us to build ourselves up when praying, so why wouldn't he want us to have this gift? When we talked about being filled with the Spirit we looked at Luke 11:9–13, where Jesus makes plain the Father wants to give us the Holy Spirit. In the Sermon on the Mount, he says, "If you, then, though you are evil, know how to give good gifts to your children, how much more will your Father in heaven give *good gifts* to those who ask him!" (Matt. 7:11). If Paul wants every one of us to have this gift, how much more does the Father!

ASK

We need to ask for the gift of tongues, trusting what Jesus says in Matthew 7:11. Remember, as with praying to receive the Holy Spirit, asking sometimes involves persistence. Prayers are not always answered at once but Jesus tells us strongly to "ask," "seek" and "knock" and our prayers will be heard.

STEP OUT

For all of us, there comes a point where if we want to speak in tongues, we have to step out in faith and take a risk. You have to start speaking and trust that the Holy Spirit will begin to enable the words. For some, when they begin to pray in tongues they find themselves speaking a beautiful language from the beginning. For most of us it isn't like this.

When you begin the devil will probably whisper in your ear, "You're just making this up." When he said that to us, the two of us said, "Lord, even if what I say is gobbledygook, may it be gobble-dygook to you." It may sound childish at the beginning, so don't focus on what you're saying, focus on Jesus. Your prayer language will develop and grow. You may find it helpful to pray with someone else who has this gift—not because they can give it to you (it is a gift of the Spirit!) but because as someone who knows what it's like they might be able to give encouragement.

THE EVERYDAY SUPERNATURAL

In order to illustrate some of what we've told you we want to share how we both received the gift of tongues. We want these stories to "wow" you with how dramatic, mystical and otherworldly they are. Unfortunately for that to happen we would have had to make them up. Here's the truth:

Mike

When I first read a book about the gift of tongues I desperately wanted to receive it. The book told me to confess my sins to God so there was no barrier between us, then to praise him in English and after a while, I would start praying in tongues. I did what the book said and … nothing.

It also said that people often speak in tongues when they are relaxed, so I ran an extra hot bath and added half a bottle of Radox. I confessed my sins again. I confessed sins I'd committed, sins I'd thought about committing and sins I'd only ever read about in newspapers. Nothing. God didn't take control of my mouth like I'd hoped. The bath grew cold and I thought I might as well give up.

A few days later I asked my cell group leaders if they would pray for me to receive the gift of tongues and they happily agreed. "Come and sit down," they said, "We're going to start by confessing our sins …" I thought, *Been there; done that*. They said that after confessing our sins, we should begin to praise God in English. Then they would start to speak in their prayer language and after a while one of them would touch my lips. That was my cue to start speaking in tongues. I started getting nervous. What would they do when they touched my lips and nothing happened? They'd know that God hadn't really accepted me and that I was a spiritual failure. But it was too late; I couldn't run away.

As they began to praise God in their prayer language I listened closely and it sounded beautiful. That only added to my feeling that I could never do it. It seemed like an eternity before they touched my lips but the moment finally came. I closed my eyes and said under my breath, "Shalla … balla … balla."

I waited for them to stone me for being a false tongue speaker. Instead they said, "Thank you, Lord. Give him more, God." I was amazed. They liked this? So I gave it another go, saying, "Shalla balla beela balla." They seemed to get excited at that. I'm nothing if not a showman, so I thought, *If they like that, I'll give them more*, and said, "Shalla balla beela balla boola balla." They went crazy!

For the next ten minutes they praised God in their beautiful tongues while I found as many variations of "shalla balla" as I could. Afterwards I said to them, "Was that it?" "Yes," the husband replied, "And I want you to do that every day for the rest of your life."

That seemed crazy to me. I thought, *I'm not doing* that *every day for the rest of my life!* I didn't feel like I'd received the gift of tongues, just the gift of gobbledygook.

As I walked home I felt despondent, and then I figured that if all I had was gobbledygook I may as well praise God with that. I checked no one was around and began to say these words that sounded like nonsense. After a while I felt God's presence, Jesus came really close, and I didn't care what I was saying, I was just praising. I tried it every day and after a while it began to change and grow.

Andy

I first learnt about the gift of tongues when I heard Mike preach on it. He told his story about how he received it and I thought, *That doesn't sound too hard.* I asked God to give me the gift and nothing happened. Nothing happened for four months and I found myself getting increasingly frustrated. When I look back I realise nothing happened because I just wasn't able to step out and start speaking. I have always operated out of my head (rather than my feelings), and I couldn't compute how you can open your mouth and say words you didn't know. I was trying to figure it all out in advance of doing it.

One night we were in Melbourne, Australia. In an evening meeting Mike spoke on tongues and lots of people responded to receive the gift. Including me (again!). When we were encouraged to begin to pray out I opened my mouth but I didn't—I felt I couldn't—say anything. It seemed like everyone around me started praying in angelic tongues. I thought, with great frustration, *How can I talk in a language I don't know? I don't understand.*

I wandered out of the meeting while it was still going on. I felt upset at myself and with God. Eventually I sat under a tree, I could hear the meeting still going on in the distance. Anselm of Canterbury is known to have said, "I believe in order to understand." I knew I needed to believe that God would give me the gift of tongues even if I didn't understand how it worked. I finally decided to speak and trust that whatever came out of my mouth was God. I almost physically choked out a few syllables. I have no idea what it was but I know it sounded tremendously unimpressive. I thought about Jesus and I kept going.

Unlike Mike, I didn't sense God's presence within a short period of time, but over the next few weeks I kept up praying my fragile "tongue". I had thought that if I prayed in tongues I would never doubt God again; I'd totally misunderstood how normal praying in tongues feels. And somewhere along the line, I stopped thinking about what I sounded like and just prayed.

A few years later I was speaking at a conference for young people in New Zealand. I had been speaking about being filled with the Holy Spirit and so at the end made space for people who wanted to be filled with the Holy Spirit and to pray in tongues. As people were being prayed for and others were worshipping, I prayed in tongues. Without thinking about it I ended up praying differently from how I normally would.

At the end a young guy came up to me and said, "I'm from South Africa and my family emigrated here. Did you realise you were speaking in Afrikaans when you prayed? You were saying two phrases." He repeated the exact phrases and then translated, "You were praying, 'Holy Spirit' and 'onto them'." I was gobsmacked. I believed in this gift, and then over time I've come to understand it. I think it always works that way round.

A FINAL THOUGHT

Once you have believed, asked and started to step out there is one final ingredient. Use it.

Like any language, when we begin we only know the ABCs; the language has to be practised in order to grow. This is the only way you'll be able to receive and enjoy all the blessings that come from praying in tongues. If you bought some aspirin for a headache and just carried it around in your pocket you'd be foolish to expect to feel better. The gift of tongues isn't something that we want to receive so we can carry it around in our pocket. It won't build us up unless we exercise it.

Never forget that ultimately the gift of tongues isn't a thing we do, it's a conversation we have with a person. It's a form of prayer; it's all about relationship. And as we practise, it will transform us.

7

HEARING GOD SPEAK PART I: BEING SHEEP

My sheep listen to my voice.

John 10:27

It may seem obvious to talk of the importance of listening to God, but it's one thing to *know* something is important, and it's another to *live* like something is important. We all *know* that eating five fruit and veg a day is important but how many of us try to get away with counting the gherkin in a cheeseburger as one of those? We can't just talk as though listening to God matters, we need to live it out too. This is key for our everyday discipleship as well as when it comes to the gift of prophecy.

MY SHEEP HEAR MY VOICE

In John 10:27 Jesus tells us that, "My sheep hear my voice, and I know them, and they follow me" (ESV). The only qualification we need to hear the voice of God is to be a sheep! The main way that

God speaks today is through the Bible—this is where his voice has ultimate authority.

Yet whilst the Bible itself makes plain that God also speaks in lots of other ways, many of us struggle to recognise what these other ways are. We tend to think that the only ways God might speak outside of the Bible are otherworldly, mystical and elusive. One of the keys to the everyday supernatural is increasingly learning to recognise the everyday whispers of our Father. For each of us this is a journey.

We want to begin by sharing some of our own stories of learning to hear God speak, not because your story will mirror ours, everyone is different, but to show how normal hearing God's voice can be. If God can speak to the two of us he can speak to anyone! Towards the end of the chapter we'll chat through some practical and biblical lessons you can begin to practise.

Mike

Not long after I began leading the youth work at St Andrew's, Chorleywood, I started to think that the career path for Christian ministry was to start as the youth pastor and then "graduate" to work with the grown-ups. After three years I went to my boss and said, "I've done three years with the young people, I think it's time I was promoted to work with the adults." After much thought he agreed. It was decided I would start the new role at the beginning of September when the new youth worker would arrive to take my place. My vicar said he was going to appoint me to be the assistant to the associate vicar, and I was very pleased until they issued me with my business card. My heart sank as I read, "Mike Pilavachi, Ass. to Ass. Vicar". It all went downhill from there.

Within days I knew I'd made the biggest mistake of my life. Working with adults was like living in slow motion. I missed the young people terribly. After six months I was desperate. "This job doesn't fit me," I said to myself. "I can't go back to the old job and I can't see what lies ahead." I felt naked and vulnerable.

One of my colleagues, Barry Kissell, was invited to speak at a youth conference in France and he asked if I would go to keep him company. After our first dinner with the French pastors we all decided to pray together. In the middle of the prayer time one of the pastors got up and started walking to the door. I watched, wondering if he was leaving. Instead he went to a coat stand and picked up a little girl's coat. I wondered what on earth he was doing as he turned around and brought the coat back to the table. I grew even more concerned when I realised he was walking straight towards me.

He stood in front of me, opened the little girl's coat and commanded, "Put it on." I knew I wouldn't even get my fingers in those sleeves. I looked up at him and said, "I can't." He said a second time, "Put the coat on." I looked over at Barry for some support, but being the man of faith that he is, he closed his eyes and carried on praying! I knew I was on my own with this crazy Frenchman.

After a while I thought, *I'll try and meet him halfway.* I ostentatiously tried to put my fingers in the sleeve. After a moment I took my hand out again and said, "You see, I can't put the coat on." "Why not?" he asked. I sighed inside. "Because it doesn't fit," I replied. "Exactly," he said, "Stop trying to put the old coat back on; the old coat doesn't fit you anymore. You're between coats—between ministries—and you want to run back to the old coat, the old ministry, because you are feeling naked and vulnerable. The Lord says, 'Trust me, Mike. Wait for me, and I will give you a new coat and a new ministry that will fit you for the next season of your life.'"

I was stunned. *How could he know this about me?* I asked myself. *Did someone tip him off?* I soon realised there was no way he could have known. God had used him to speak to me prophetically.

Straightaway I started to read the Bible and saw things I had never seen before.

I realised it was full of God speaking prophetically to people. God spoke to a wandering nomad called Abraham (Gen. 12:1–3; 15:1–21; 17:1–22; 18:16–33), he spoke to Joseph through dreams (Gen. 37:1–11), he spoke to Moses at a burning bush (Exod. 3:4–4:22), he spoke to Gideon through a fleece (Judg. 6:36–40), he spoke to Samuel when he was a little boy in the tabernacle (1 Sam. 3:1–14), and so on.

There is a whole section of books in the Old Testament called the Prophets, that are a record of God speaking to Israel (Isaiah to Malachi). Then I turned to the Gospels. I saw that Jesus regularly spent time in prayer before receiving his marching orders from his Father (such as in Mark 1:35, Luke 4:42 and Luke 6:12). In John 5:19 Jesus said he only did what he saw his Father doing. And elsewhere, that he spoke only the words his Father gave him to speak (John 12:49–50). When I turned to the Acts of the Apostles, I saw numerous examples of a church directed by God through the gift of prophecy (e.g., Acts 5:1–5; 8:26–30; 9:3–15).

Then I turned to the letters. One verse leaped out and punched me: 1 Corinthians 14:1, "Follow the way of love and eagerly desire gifts of the Spirit, especially prophecy."

That was it—I was going to eagerly desire the gift of prophecy! I went into my room, closed the curtains (because I have always believed it's more holy in the dark) and I said, "Lord, give me a prophecy now." And then I waited. After rather a long time the only thing that came into my mind was *Spaghetti*. I wondered, *What can I do prophetically with this?* I could point to someone and say, "Bolognese," to another person, "Carbonara," but after a while unless the person was Italian it wasn't going to mean anything. I said to myself, "I've eagerly desired the gift of prophecy, I haven't received it so I'll just get on with life." So I gave up.

Stepping Out (Reluctantly ...)

A few weeks later our church hosted a retreat for church leaders. I heard that on the last evening a vicar called Bruce Collins (who was, I was told, "prophetically gifted") would come with a "prophetically gifted" assistant. They were going to prophesy over everyone in turn. I was intrigued so I sat at the back and watched. I was, quite frankly, amazed. Many times they would say things to the leaders who would respond with joy and astonishment.

At the end I approached Bruce and said, "How did you do that? When I tried, all I got was 'spaghetti'." He said, "How do you expect God to speak to you?" I thought about it and realised I had been waiting for a booming voice calling out, "Hear ye! Hear ye! God calling Mike. Are you receiving me? Tablet of stone on its way down. Duck!" Bruce said, "Mike, God speaks in a whisper not a shout." Then after a moment's pause he said, "We're doing this again in six weeks' time, why don't you come and be my assistant and we can prophesy together?"

I immediately agreed and thought, *I have six weeks to become holy*. I decided I would pray every day for those six weeks. I would read my Bible every day for those six weeks. I would fast every day for those six weeks (between meals—that's how I do my fasting). And at the end I would be a spiritual superman, ready to prophesy life-changing words at the drop of a hat. But, of course, I forgot.

One morning I woke up, checked my diary and sat bolt upright as I realised it was the day when I was supposed to become a prophet. I sat there and thought, *I don't feel very prophetic*. I looked in the mirror and thought, *I don't look very prophetic. I look more pathetic than prophetic. I need to practise.*

I went to Sainsbury's and I asked the Lord to give me prophetic words for strangers. All I managed to do was frighten a lot of elderly people as I followed them around, waiting for a word for them. I went home and imagined a nightmare scenario: Bruce and I would pray and then he would have amazing prophetic words for everyone. Then Bruce and everyone else would turn to me and say, "What do you have, Mike?" and I would have to say, "Not a lot." My great fear was that I would go down as the first prophet in the history of the church who never had a prophecy.

I started making bargains with God. *If you give me one prophecy, Lord, I'll do anything you want.* Then I thought, *If I don't get the gift of prophecy, perhaps I could try the gift of guessing.* I quickly dismissed that idea! I even prayed that I would get ill so I wouldn't have to go to the meeting.

Eventually, with a heavy heart, I left for the meeting. When I arrived Bruce motioned for me to sit next to him and soon the first couple was sitting in front of us, waiting to hear from God. Bruce and I prayed and waited. I was desperate. The only thing that came into my mind was the song "Dancing Queen", by ABBA. I wondered if this was Satan. The more I tried not to think of the song, the more the lyrics pounded in my skull. Bruce began to prophesy and then, as in my nightmare, he turned to me and said, "What do you have, Mike?" I knew that if I said nothing then I would *never* have the courage to say anything.

More in fear than faith, I looked at the pastor's wife and mumbled, "I wonder if the Lord wants to say to you, in the words of ABBA, 'You can dance, you can jive, having the time of your life.'" I felt a complete fool. The couple started laughing and I was ready to walk out. Then the wife said, "Three weeks ago I started a dance group in my church for the worship times, and as we were driving here tonight I said to my husband, 'I'm going to cancel the dance group. What was I thinking starting it?' I shook my head and said to him, 'I can't dance. I can't dance.'" I was totally shocked. Never in my wildest dreams did I think that God would want to speak using the lyrics of a Swedish pop group.

The main lesson I learnt is that you never know if it's God until you say it. After that night with Bruce I began a journey of learning to hear God speak and I've found that God speaks in many different ways and rarely is it loud. It's often as gentle as a butterfly landing and taking off again, and the only way you find out if it is the Lord speaking is by saying it, humbly and with love. Sharing a word is always a risk, no matter how long you've been doing it, but I have been amazed at how many times God has spoken in the most ordinary of ways.

I've also noticed that God speaks to different people in different ways. We have different personalities and interests and God knows how to speak to us in our own language. He speaks to me and Andy differently and he'll speak to you in a unique way too.

Andy

My story is very different from Mike's. When we first started doing ministry together I would get extremely frustrated. Mike had been practising the gift of prophecy for a long time and it seemed to me as if he had an instant connection to heaven. I felt as if I'd maxed-out my data allowance and had been cut off. I never seemed to hear God. I can remember time and time again saying to Mike, "Why doesn't God ever speak to me? You seem to hear him so clearly—how do you do that?"

At certain moments I would gear myself up, concentrate hard and "listen" for God's voice. I'm sure I looked like I was constipated; that's certainly how it felt! Nothing remotely spiritual happened. I would either have a total mind blank or end up thinking the most bizarre thoughts. Once when waiting for a prophetic word I found myself calculating how much water would fit in a yellow rubber glove before it exploded.

As I look back I see that I was treating prophecy like a code I was trying to crack. I've always operated from my head. If only I could concentrate hard enough for long enough, I'd get the right sequence of numbers in the right order and solve the puzzle. But the months went by and it never happened. Mike and many others had amazing prophecies around me and I felt like a failure. I began to quietly lose hope. Any expectation that God might speak to me quickly died.

I was waiting for my "ABBA song" moment. I thought it would happen the same way for me as it did for Mike. Instead God surprised me; it's as if he sneaked up when I wasn't looking and began to speak to me in ways I hadn't expected.

Towards the end of my gap year I found myself reading the Bible and noticing things that I'd never seen before. A verse I'd read many times would strike me as significant. Sometimes I'd notice a theme or a connection between a few different passages. Occasionally things would jump off the page like they were truths I was reading for the first time. It didn't feel spectacular or "spiritual" I just got enthusiastic about something I'd noticed. I would go to Mike and excitedly say, "Isn't Jesus amazing when he does such and such?" or "I've never noticed it before but don't you love this passage on forgiveness?" Then one day Mike looked at me, smiled, and said, "Gosh, that's quite a good point for someone who never hears God."

I was expecting God to speak one way and he began by speaking another. I shouldn't have been surprised he was speaking to me through the Bible but I think there's a part of me that thought that was cheating. I thought it needed to feel more supernatural than that.

That was the beginning, and the best way I can describe it is I grew into it. When I first met my wife, Beth, she was a complete mystery to me. I couldn't begin to understand what went through her head. She would say things that didn't make sense. She would drop hints that I would never pick up. But over the months, as I got to know her better, I started to notice signals that I hadn't even realised were there. For example, when she said, "No, don't worry about buying me some chocolate," what she *really* meant was, "Buy me the biggest bar in the shop and insist that I eat it all tonight."

We grow in hearing God speak as we grow in relationship with him. As we get to know him we start to hear whispers where before there seemed to have been none. I began to realise that prophecy isn't a thing; it's not a code or a puzzle. Prophecy is about a relationship with a person. The more familiar we become with Jesus, the easier it is to notice his promptings.

Hearing in the Ordinary

After some time, I began to notice God was speaking to me through books. Again it's normal, ordinary and unspectacular but it was his voice nonetheless. I've always enjoyed reading but I began to find that I'd pick a book off a shelf, seemingly at random, and it would end up speaking profoundly into what was going on in my life at that time. This didn't happen all the time, and as you read this it may seem like mere coincidence, but it's happened so frequently that it's now something I expect. I see God's hand behind it.

I remember praying one week about what to speak on at church and the thought came into my head that I should speak on death. I'd never given a talk on death in my life and I was pretty reluctant to start then! The very next thing that happened was I noticed a book on my shelf called *Our Greatest Gift*, by Henri Nouwen. It had been there for years; I'd never opened it and can't remember how I even got it. I suddenly had a sense I needed to read it. I said aloud, "If that book is on death then that's what I'll speak on." To my amazement the whole book was a meditation on death and dying.

When I look back I wonder if God began to help me join the dots with scriptures and books to encourage me that I wasn't totally deaf to his voice.

As I began to grow in confidence that God was speaking to me I started to practise prophecy a little more. When I look back, one of the things that surprises me is how unspiritual it felt. I had always assumed, when I'd heard other people's stories, that something akin to electricity had raced through their body and they had announced a message that had just been burned into their souls.

When I started to practise it didn't work like that. I went through a season of trying to have a prophecy a day for somebody. I'd sit in my room at university and ask God to give me a word for someone. Usually, after a while, someone would come to mind and I'd get a Bible verse, a picture or something else. I still wasn't feeling confident, so I decided to text people the prophecies—it saved me the embarrassment of getting them wrong face to face! I did this for two or three weeks and I'm pretty certain that I sent out a lot of "blessed thoughts" rather than prophecies. Most of my texts went something like, "I see a waterfall and God says he loves you …"

Then one day God brought to mind a friend who I hadn't been in touch with for months. In my mind I saw a picture of an apple with a bite taken out of it. I texted her the picture and a message that I thought went with it, "You've only taken one bite out of your life and the Lord wants you to know that there is so much more to enjoy." It felt pretty simple, but she texted right back, "That's amazing, thank you so much." She explained she had been due to get married but about nine months before had broken off the engagement. I didn't realise it, but that was the very day she would have been walking down the aisle.

Depending on God

Another way that God has been training me to hear him has to do with giving talks. (I'm aware most of us aren't going to be working for churches and preaching, but hopefully you can connect with the principle.)

I am a control freak. Whilst Mike seems to have an ability to meander through life not planning too far in advance, I have a chronic inability to do anything that I'm not certain will be a success. I plan and scheme and perfect until I'm sure something is good enough. I don't take risks lightly. God began challenging me to trust him more with preaching.

One morning I was praying and said to the Lord, "How can I trust you more? Is there anything I can do to depend on you?" To my surprise a thought came into my head: *Don't prepare your talk for tonight until just before you go.* I was due to speak at a celebration at church that evening. At the time I wished I hadn't asked the question—for me not preparing is like Mike not eating. On this occasion I decided to obey, I think because I was just desperate to be closer to God.

I had planned to spend the whole day preparing, instead I spent most of it pacing around and banging my head against a wall "in faith". Then finally an hour or so before I had to leave I sat down with a blank piece of paper: "Seriously, God, you had better come through for me!" I prayed as I started to try to scribble out the talk.

I wish you could have met me as I walked home that night. I was floating on air. If you'd heard the talk you may have wondered what I was so happy about! It was fine but not great. But I was ecstatic because I had stood on a stage in front of hundreds of people, with a few scribbles and a Bible, and I had experienced an intimacy with God I'd never known before. It was just the two of us; we were a team. I had no choice in that moment but to depend on him. And I—a control freak—loved it.

Don't misunderstand; God wasn't saying he never wanted me—or anyone else—to prepare talks. It was a particular command for me for that particular day that was about me trusting in and relying on him in a new way. The point was that he had spoken to me and I had responded.

Taking Baby Steps

Of course, hearing from God continues to be a gradual process. Some years ago I was in one of the main meetings at Soul Survivor. There were about ten thousand young people there and at the end of a talk we invited the Holy Spirit to come and meet us. As we all stood in silence I remember asking, *Lord, what do you want to do?*

My plan was to hear what God wanted, then wait and see if Mike got the same thing. Mike can be wrong, of course, but he's far more experienced than I am and I was practising. The word *healing* came into my head. A few minutes later Mike announced what he thought the Lord was beginning to do—it was something completely different. *Oh well*, I sighed to myself. *Wrong again. I'll try again tomorrow.*

A little later I began to walk around the back of the Big Top to watch what God was doing. As I stood there I spotted a young guy and had a sense that I should go and pray for him. I dismissed it, thinking, *Now you're getting desperate.* But it wouldn't go away so I wandered over and introduced myself. "Would you mind if I prayed for you?" "Sure," he said. "Is there anything in particular I can pray for?" I asked. "Yes, healing," he replied.

He explained that he only had one kidney, it was only working at 30 per cent and he was due to go into hospital shortly for an operation. I was amazed; it had felt like such a throw away thought on stage, and the sense to pray for him was something I'd have dismissed nine times out of ten. Some of his friends gathered around and we began to pray. After a few minutes the Holy Spirit started to rest on him powerfully and he was clearly meeting God in a very tangible way.

I was so encouraged—God hadn't spoken to me for the ten thousand but he had led me to one person in the crowd and of all the things he could have needed prayer for it was healing. The next afternoon I was doing a seminar and I shared what had happened. As I was telling the story a large man got to his feet and started to walk towards me. There were about eight hundred people in the venue and I starting thinking, *Oh no, this guy must be crazy, he wants to correct my theology in front of everybody.* I kept talking as he walked closer.

Finally, when he was standing right beside me, I had to stop. I turned to him and saw he was crying and shaking. It had taken everything in him to walk up in front of everyone. He said, "I had to come and tell you that the guy you prayed for last night was my son. He was really scared because of the operation and he really needed to meet with God. Thank you." Then he walked out.

I almost lost it right there and then. I was overwhelmed with God's kindness, I'd found out (almost by accident) that the boy and his dad were incredibly blessed, and I was massively encouraged. It was as if God was seizing the moment to say, "Keep going, Andy, Keep taking the risks and practising. It is me."

A GUIDE TO HEARING GOD SPEAK

As we've said, God speaks to each of us in different ways but there are some essential lessons the Bible gives us on how to hear God.

GOD WANTS TO SPEAK

We instinctively know that any healthy relationship involves two-way conversation but how many of us see prayer as being only about our talking to God? We would never meet up with a friend, talk at them, and then walk away without giving them an opportunity to speak too. Friends listen to each other.

Jesus makes a staggering statement in John 15, saying, "You are my friends if you do what I command. I no longer call you servants, because a servant does not know his master's business. Instead, I have called you friends, *for everything that I learned from my Father I have made known to you*" (John 15:14–15).

Obedience is key to friendship with God, but before we obey, we first need to listen. It is a huge declaration from Jesus that *he wants* to share all the family secrets with his friends. He actually says, "*Everything.*"

Let's just stop for a moment. We could lie down and ponder these words for three weeks and still not fully grasp them. "*Everything that I learned from my Father I have made known to you.*"

Now, have a stiff drink and carry on reading.

We need to learn the art of two-way conversation so that we can hear all that Jesus wants to share with us. He makes it plain that he is more than willing to speak; we don't have to twist his arm as we sometimes think we do. One of his titles is "The Word". If we're not hearing from God, the problem is not at his end!

Samuel is a model for us in this; when he was a little boy in the tabernacle he heard the Lord calling his name. His response was, "Speak, for your servant is listening" (1 Sam. 3:10). Many of us reverse those words: "Listen, Lord, your servant is speaking ..." Let us adopt Samuel's approach. Prayer isn't simply about talking at God; it involves learning the art of listening to him too.

"DIALLING DOWN"

Listening to God is more than simply sitting in silence. The secret lies in learning to still our hearts. That doesn't necessarily mean going to a monastery or up a mountain (though Jesus regularly went up mountains or into deserts in order to pray). You can have a "noisy heart" when you are all alone and a "still heart" sitting on a crowded tube. Sometimes getting away from others can be helpful but that isn't the main point. We are talking about a kind of inward attentiveness. A "portable sanctuary of the heart", as Richard Foster called it.[1] This is to do with a state of mind, an inner stillness of the soul, whether alone or among people.

This inner attentiveness is less about striving and more about resting and being. It comes when we "dial down", relax and sit quietly in God's presence knowing that we have every right to be there.

Psalm 46:10 talks of this in saying, "Be still, and know that I am God." Psalm 131:1–2 also describes what this might feel like: "My heart is not proud, LORD, my eyes are not haughty; I do not concern myself with great matters or things too wonderful for me. But I have calmed and quieted myself, I am like a weaned child with its mother; like a weaned child I am content."

Whilst much of the language of the Psalms is about stirring ourselves to worship God, many other verses speak of stillness and being ready to hear God's whisper. As we said, it can feel as gentle as a butterfly landing on your shoulder and taking off again. This isn't just our experience; it seems to be the experience of God's people throughout history.

In 1 Kings 18 Elijah won a great victory against the prophets of Baal. He then fled for his life and found himself exhausted and demoralised in a cave on Mount Horeb, waiting to encounter God. We can read what happened in 1 Kings 19:11–13:

> The LORD said, "Go out and stand on the mountain in the presence of the LORD, for the LORD is about to pass by."
>
> Then a great and powerful wind tore the mountains apart and shattered the rocks before the LORD, but the LORD was not in the wind. After the wind there was an earthquake, but the LORD was not in the earthquake. After the earthquake came a fire, but the LORD was not in the fire. And after the fire came a gentle whisper. When Elijah heard it, he pulled his cloak over his face and went out and stood at the mouth of the cave.

The Lord was not in the earthquake, wind or fire, but in the gentle whisper. This is how he speaks to his friends. Is there enough stillness in our hearts to hear that whisper?

PRACTISING STILLNESS

For this to be more than just a theory we need to make sure we take practical steps to build stillness into our lives. It won't just happen by itself. If this is something you want to develop why not consider doing some of the following? Start small if it feels overwhelming.

- **Read the Bible each day.** This is the key way you will hear God speaking.
- **Pray each day,** being sure to leave a time of silence before God.
- **Keep a journal** of things you feel like God is speaking to you about.
- **Make the most of times alone.** Most of our days are filled with people and we cram the rest of them with noise—music, TV, the Internet. But our days also have little spaces in them, perhaps when you are walking to work or school, when you wake up or just before you go to sleep. Find a place at home or elsewhere where you can be still for a short time.

We need to still our hearts in the midst of life's busyness that we might learn to discern his voice. So often we ask God to speak to us not realising that he is *always* speaking. The key is not in asking God to speak louder but in our becoming quieter.

As we've told our stories we've been trying to communicate how surprisingly "ordinary" the voice of God is. The only qualification we need is to be a sheep. That's a pretty low bar! God will speak to you through everyday things. Much of the time we *are* in fact hearing him; it just often doesn't look how we expected it to. In the next chapter we're going to be more specific and look at the gift of prophecy but it was important to start here as prophecy flourishes when the whole of our relationship with God is defined by two-way conversation.

8

HEARING GOD SPEAK PART II: PRACTISING PROPHECY

Follow the way of love and eagerly desire gifts of the Spirit,
especially prophecy.

1 Corinthians 14:1

The gift of prophecy is a unique way in which we hear and communicate a revelation from God. For the sake of ease, we are going to deliberately blur the line between prophecy and "words of knowledge" (1 Cor. 12:8) as these are so similar.

WHAT IS THE GIFT OF PROPHECY?

In the New Testament the term *prophecy* can have a broad range of meanings. It is associated with preaching and evangelism, both spontaneous preaching and well-thought-out pastoral teaching. On the day of Pentecost, for example, the disciples were filled with the Spirit, spilled out into the streets and Peter (inarticulate at the best of times) preached. Three thousand people became Christians!

Here we want to focus on prophecy defined as the gift or ability to receive and communicate supernatural revelation for a group, individual or situation. It is knowledge that we would not have were it not for God divinely giving it to us. (Think of the examples we gave before of hearing God speak through ABBA lyrics and a picture of an apple.) As we'll see it's a huge privilege and a blessing to play a part in God speaking to someone. If the gift of tongues edifies us, the gift of prophecy builds up the church: "I would like every one of you to speak in tongues, but I would rather have you prophesy" (1 Cor. 14:5). Our hope is that by the time you finish this chapter you'll be ready to use prophecy to begin building up those around you.

THE BIBLE AND PROPHECY

The Bible reveals all ultimate truth about God. Within that context the gift of prophecy can give specific revelation for a particular situation. In football there are clearly defined rules and boundaries that apply to any football match, anywhere. Scripture is a little like that, it provides the clearly defined truth of Christianity. This truth applies to any church, believer and situation.

Within a football match, however, there may also be tactical calls that are specific for that particular game. The coach might assess the Arsenal defence and decide only one striker is necessary (most coaches playing Arsenal do decide that). Prophecies are a little like the tactical calls in a game. They cannot, and must not, override the truths of the Bible, but within that context they can be incredibly helpful. To quote Michael Green, "Prophecy is not the equivalent of Scripture. Prophecy is a particular word for a particular congregation at a particular time through a particular person. Scripture is for all Christians in all places at all times."[1]

Scripture is *always* God's Word, but prophecies need to be weighed and tested. They will at times be wrong; sometimes people may say what they want to be true rather than something that is from God. For instance, if someone says to you, "God told me we are going to be married, have seven children and live in Slough" it doesn't mean you need to buy the ring. Prophecy is an amazing gift with incredible potential to bless the church, and the response to any misuse of a gift is not disuse but correct use. We want to encourage you with all we have to pursue this gift because *Scripture itself* teaches this is what we should be doing: "Follow the way of love and eagerly desire gifts of the Spirit, *especially prophecy*" (1 Cor. 14:1).

THE "PROPHETHOOD" OF ALL BELIEVERS

We believe prophecy is a gift available for all of us. We talked in chapter 5 about how the New Testament makes a distinction between ministries and gifts. Not all of us will have the ministry of a prophet but all of us, however unspiritual and inadequate we might feel, can learn to practise the gift of prophecy. Neither of us has ever felt very "ready" or "prophetic" but we have been amazed at what God has done despite this. This is part of the joy and the adventure of the everyday supernatural.

In his book *More*, Simon Ponsonby writes, "Moses on one occasion declared, 'I would that all God's people were prophets' (Num. 11:29). At Pentecost his desire became a reality."[2] When the Spirit was given Peter stood to preach to the crowd. Of all the passages he could have chosen on the day the church was birthed, he chose Joel 2:28–32. Joel prophesied about the outpouring of the Holy Spirit on "all flesh". He makes clear that a sign of this outpouring is that the "sons and daughters" and the "male and female servants" would begin to prophesy. Elsewhere the New Testament speaks of the priesthood of all believers, but "Pentecost actually points to the *prophethood* of all believers. The tongues of fire, which rested on each of them, set their tongues on fire."[3]

The same Spirit can set our tongues ablaze. We have the presence of God inside us and where God's presence is there his power is also. So let's get practical and look at why the gift of prophecy is given to us and how we can begin to exercise it.

WHY IS PROPHECY GIVEN?

If we want to begin to use any tool, the most basic thing to know is what it's actually for. We don't want to use a wrench to hammer in a nail. If prophecy is a tool for us to use, what is its purpose?

TO GLORIFY JESUS

Prophecy is given that Jesus might be glorified. In Revelation 19:10 we read, "It is the Spirit of prophecy who bears testimony to Jesus." This means many things but one of them is that Jesus is revealed through prophecy. Not every prophecy is a statement about Jesus, but true prophecy will cause us to know and love Jesus more. New Testament prophecy is more about revealing Jesus than it is about revealing the future. (Although God may speak to us about things that haven't yet happened, prophecy is not the Christian version of fortune telling.)

When the crazy French pastor went up to Mike with the little girl's coat, Mike's response wasn't, "What an amazing French pastor! I want to follow you." It was, "What an amazing Jesus! You know all about my life; I love you even more."

TO STRENGTHEN, ENCOURAGE AND COMFORT

1 Corinthians 14:3 tells us that "the one who prophesies speaks to people for their strengthening, encouraging and comfort." Does the church still need to be strengthened, encouraged and comforted? We think it does! This is why the gift of prophecy matters.

The book of Acts is filled with people exercising the gift of prophecy. We read one example of many in Acts 9:10–15:

> In Damascus there was a disciple named Ananias. The Lord called to him in a vision, "Ananias!"
>
> "Yes, Lord," he answered.
>
> The Lord told him, "Go to the house of Judas on Straight Street and ask for a man from Tarsus named Saul, for he is praying. In a vision he has seen a man named Ananias come and place his hands on him to restore his sight."

"Lord," Ananias answered, "I have heard many reports about this man and all the harm he has done to your holy people in Jerusalem. And he has come here with authority from the chief priests to arrest all who call on your name."

But the Lord said to Ananias, "Go! This man is my chosen instrument to proclaim my name to the Gentiles and their kings and to the people of Israel."

In this story the Lord speaks to both Ananias and Saul. It's easy to understand why Ananias was reluctant—Saul had been dragging believers to jail and had been heading to Damascus to do more damage. He was a formidable enemy of the church. Eventually the Lord was able to persuade Ananias that he (God) might know more about what was happening than Ananias gave him credit for. Still, can you imagine how Ananias must have felt wandering down Straight Street and knocking on Saul's door?

Saul on the other hand had been sitting inside, supernaturally blinded for three days. After his encounter with Jesus on the road to Damascus he would surely have been repenting and wondering, "What next?" He also must have been thinking, "Will I ever see again?" Cue the vision and the instruction from God to wait for a man named Ananias.

To both men God supernaturally revealed something about a particular person. There was no way they could have humanly known what was shown to them. What a moment it must have been when the blinded persecutor opened the door, the scales fell from his eyes, and Ananias baptised him. We're pretty sure that both Ananias and Saul were strengthened, encouraged and comforted by this gift of prophecy. Saul went on to become Paul—the apostle to the Gentiles. What might have been missed without this revelation?

Perhaps it's no coincidence then that it was Paul himself who later underlined the value of prophecy to the Corinthians: "Anyone who speaks in a tongue edifies themselves, but the one who prophesies edifies the church. I would like every one of you to speak in tongues, but I would rather have you prophesy" (1 Cor. 14:4–5).

Mike

To give another example, in 2004 we ran a mission in London called Soul in the City, where I worked closely with my friends Roy Crowne (national director of Youth for Christ) and Andy Hawthorne (The Message Trust). After the mission we met in the summer of 2005 in order to talk and pray about whether we should continue to work together in encouraging mission in the church.

We met on the balcony of the speakers' lounge at Soul Survivor. Through the glass door I noticed an elderly friend of mine, Terry Ackrill, with unique prophetic gifts come and sit down. I suddenly thought it would be fun to ask Terry to pray for Roy and Andy, so I took them inside and introduced them. They were a little frustrated because they wanted to get on with the meeting. Terry began to pray for them and then stopped and said, "I feel the Lord is saying that I shouldn't pray for just the two of them. I should pray for the three of you because the Lord says he wants you to work together in encouraging the church in mission."

We were stunned. Terry had no idea why we were meeting and that that was the very question we were trying to answer. Needless to say, all three of us were strengthened, encouraged and comforted. God had a plan and we were on the right track. As an added bonus that one prophetic word saved months of committee meetings!

HOW DOES PROPHECY WORK?

RIDDLES—THE LOVE LANGUAGE OF PROPHECY

In Numbers 12:6–8 Moses's brother and sister had been talking behind his back. God became angry and summoned them before him, saying,

> When there is a prophet among you,
>   I, the LORD, reveal myself to them in visions,
>   I speak to them in dreams.
> But this is not true of my servant Moses;
>   he is faithful in all my house.
> With him I speak face to face,
>   clearly and not in riddles;
>   he sees the form of the LORD.

So, unless you're Moses, this verse makes it obvious that God will not always speak clearly. Often he speaks softly and in riddles. He will reveal something supernaturally to us, but it's always something we need to pay close attention to. We usually need to then carefully interpret and apply what we hear. We are convinced that God's motivation behind this—as with all he does—is to draw us into relationship. As we have said repeatedly, God doesn't want us to exercise these gifts apart from him, but with him.

When God gives us a prophecy he is giving us an invitation to come closer. To fully understand a prophecy, we often need to ask questions and ponder the application with him. Of course all of this can take place in just moments, but when we have these moments again and again, our friendship with God comes alive in a new way.

REVELATION, INTERPRETATION AND APPLICATION

Many of us think that prophecy is simply receiving a revelation. While it begins with a revelation it is more than that.

Sometimes we need to ask, "Lord, what do you mean by this revelation?" In other words, "What is the interpretation?" For example: if we see a picture of a balloon, we could just say, "I see a balloon." Or we could ask the Lord for more, "Is there a party? Does someone work for a balloon factory? Is it about rising up?"

We also need to think carefully about application. So often we get into trouble because we don't ask the Lord how we can apply a prophetic word. It can be helpful to ask the Lord, "Do you want me to say this now and how do you want me to say it?" We have come across prophetic words that have damaged a church because they have been applied in the wrong way or have been shared without love and without humility.

Some time ago we heard a story that illustrates this perfectly. A visiting "prophet" was preaching at a church in the United States. In the middle of the service he pointed to someone and said, "I believe the Lord is saying you have been embezzling from your company and stealing money from them." The church was horrified—not least the accused! He protested his innocence; he was a long-established elder in the church and much respected. A public argument ensued between the prophet and the elder until the pastor had the wisdom to stop the meeting and invite both of them to join him in his study. He asked the prophet, "What exactly did you see?" He replied, "I saw a man with a robber's mask over his eyes and an old-fashioned loot bag with a dollar sign on it. He was leaving an office with a bag full of loot." The pastor asked, "Is that all you saw? Could there be another interpretation?"

The elder ran a business in partnership with another man who was responsible for the accounts of the business. They decided to invite a firm of accountants to do a special audit of the company finances. It turned out that the partner had been secretly taking money out of the company. If it had carried on much longer the company would have been bankrupt. The interpretation of the revelation was actually a warning to this man about his business partner, but the "prophet" made a false assumption. We would also suggest that the application was terrible. He should have gone to the man privately and spoken to him instead of publicly humiliating him. We grow in maturity in the gift of prophecy when we learn to discern the interpretation and application of any revelation.

Like Jesus we need to speak the words the Father gives us to speak (John 12:49) and be sensitive as to when and how to say them (John 16:12). As you begin to exercise this gift you may find it helpful to hold what we have said about revelation, interpretation and application at the back of your mind.

HOW WILL GOD SPEAK TO ME?

Most of the time God speaks very gently. One size does not fit all and although we are about to outline a number of ways that God might speak to you, it is by no means an exhaustive list. We are cautious about being too prescriptive as these are not rules. Prophecy is not about learning techniques, it is, as with all the gifts, about relationship. If we reduce the gift of prophecy to a particular technique, then we usually stop depending on God and we start relying on our human formula.

Below is a list of suggestions for how God might speak as you begin to listen. As we might expect they are normal, everyday ways. Whilst there are clear biblical examples for many of these suggestions, we should not expect there to always be an exact example. At times it is impossible to know the manner in which God was speaking to some of the individuals in Acts (we're not told what was going on in their minds, emotions and so on). However, we believe the Bible makes it clear that God speaks in a variety of ways and that as Lord of Creation he can speak to his people however he chooses. As you read through the list you may want to pray and ask God to highlight one particular way that he wants to start to speak to you.

YOU SEE IT

Pictures and Visions

After the coming of the Holy Spirit at Pentecost there are lots of instances of visions. Paul had one at his conversion (Acts 9:3–7), as Stephen was being killed he saw a vision of Jesus (Acts 7:55–60), Peter's commission to the Gentiles involved a vision (Acts 10:9–16; 11:4–8) and Paul's call to Macedonia came through a vision (Acts 16:6–10).

There are varying degrees of "vision". They can range from angelic visitations and trances (see Acts 10:3, 10) (something neither of us has yet experienced) to something that feels totally normal. Often it is just a case of something flashing into the "screen" of our mind. Try to picture Big Ben—that's what we mean by the screen of our mind. It is that normal and everyday. Sometimes we dismiss these things because we think our own imaginations are producing them or they seem too simple.

Growing in the everyday supernatural involves understanding that God works and speaks through our human faculties. Next time this happens, rather than assume it's nothing, begin to chat to God. "Is this you? What does it mean?" Share it with the person you are praying for and see if it speaks to them.

Andy

I remember having lunch with someone who was visiting us from the United States. We were chatting about nothing in particular when he suddenly gave me a strange look. He gestured towards me and said, "I see you with a suit of armour resting over your chest. I feel like

God is going to move you into a new level of authority in what you're doing." He encouraged me about what was coming in the future and then we carried on eating and chatting.

Over the next few weeks various people came up to me with similar words or pictures and I realised God was saying something. I was completely in awe of this guy. I thought, *He* sees *God's messages on people. Wow. If only it could be that easy for me.* When I asked God to give me a prophecy a day (as mentioned in the previous chapter) he would often speak to me through a picture that would come to mind. It felt much less spiritual than I was expecting and certainly much less spiritual than when I was on the receiving end of a picture God had given someone else.

———————————

Much of what we have learned about the everyday supernatural has come from someone called John Wimber. He was a pastor in California who experienced a lot of God's supernatural power in his daily life. Here's a story he used to tell of God speaking to him on a plane:

> Shortly after takeoff, I pushed back the reclining seat and adjusted the seat belt, preparing to relax. My eyes wandered around the cabin, not looking at anything in particular. Seated across from me was a middle-aged man, a businessman to judge from his appearance, but there was nothing unusual or noteworthy about him. But in the split second that

my eyes happened to be cast in his direction, I saw
something that startled me.

Written across his face in very clear and distinct
letters I thought I saw the word *adultery*. I blinked,
rubbed my eyes, and looked again. It was still there.
Adultery. I was seeing it not with my eyes, but in
my mind's eye. No one else on the plane, I am sure,
saw it. It was the Spirit of God communicating to
me. The fact that it was a spiritual phenomenon
made it no less real.

By now the man had become aware that I was
looking at him ("gaping at him" might be a more
accurate description).

"What do you want?" he snapped.

As he spoke, a woman's name came clearly to
mind. This was more familiar to me; I had become
accustomed to the Holy Spirit bringing things to
my awareness through these kinds of promptings.

Somewhat nervously, I leaned across the aisle
and asked, "Does the name Jane [not her real name]
mean anything to you?"

His face turned ashen. "We've got to talk," he
stammered.[4]

Wimber ended up leading this person to Jesus. His story
illustrates what we mean when we say sometimes we can see God
speaking. Not always with the naked eye, but on the screen of our
minds.

YOU FEEL IT

Sometimes God will cause us to have a feeling that (if we can put it like this) isn't our feeling. We might suddenly feel a sharp pain in a part of our body that wasn't there a moment before. We might suddenly find ourselves caught up with an overwhelming emotion just for a moment. We have learnt that this can often be God speaking.

A friend of ours, Todd Atkinson, went through a season where the main way God would speak to him was through his emotions. He would suddenly begin to feel something intensely that he knew wasn't for him, it was God giving him a window into someone else's situation. He was able to find that person, pray for them, and show that God knew them intimately.

Andy

At a healing meeting we had at our church a few weeks ago the speaker gave space for people to have words of knowledge. At once I felt a tightness in my chest. I was a bit nervous about saying anything (and I'm a pastor in the church—what does that tell you?), so instead I wondered to myself about whether God was speaking.

The speaker also invited anyone who had a terminal condition to come forward for prayer. In the crowd of four hundred, one elderly gentleman made his way to the front and I went to pray for him. As I started to pray he told me that he had a disease in his lungs that meant he constantly struggled to breathe. It may seem like a small thing, but my confidence and expectancy that God was going to do something rose as I realised God had indeed been highlighting this man's condition to me before I prayed for him.

YOU SPEAK IT

Ever said something without thinking? God can sometimes speak through what we've nicknamed "automatic mouth". We open our mouths, "in faith", to say something without being totally sure what is about to come out of them. Sometimes only a few words are needed, at other times we can begin to say a few words and they can be like releasing the cork in a bottle.

The Holy Spirit is "a revealing and speaking Spirit",[5] and the disciples experienced something of this when they spoke "as the Spirit enabled them" (Acts 2:4; see also 4:8; 25, 31; 6:10; 7:55–56; 19:6; 21:4, 11; 28:24–27). Although Peter is writing about the Old Testament prophets, he alludes to what we mean here when he says, "For prophecy never had its origin in the human will, but prophets, though human, spoke from God as they were carried along by the Holy Spirit" (2 Pet. 1:21).

Let us be clear that we're not suggesting you open your mouth and make things up! We're saying that sometimes you might be praying for someone and have a strong sense that God wants you to say something but you have no idea what. Sometimes the best thing to do is begin to speak and trust God will guide your words.

A word of warning: if you don't do this willingly God may just catch you off guard …

Mike

I was speaking at a meeting of about four hundred people. At the beginning of the ministry time I had a sense that there might be someone there with a fuzzy head on the left side, like a headache. They'd had it for years, it would come and go, and they had it at the time. Honesty compels me to admit that I looked around and weighed up the odds. I thought, *Four hundred people ... chances of someone with a migraine that's more on the left hand side ... maybe, 50 per cent. I like those odds.* I then said what I'd been given.

The Lord is holy, all loving, all knowing, glorious, compassionate and kind. He can also be very sneaky. At the last moment the thought dropped into my head, *And it's got something to do with your sister.* I found myself saying it before I could work out the odds. Immediately I was cross with myself. *You idiot,* I said to myself. *You had a 50 per cent chance of getting it right and you blew it. How will anyone respond to a word like that? How can someone be getting headaches for years and it have something to do with their sister? Does their sister hit them over the head with a frying pan?*

At that point I turned around and saw a young lady standing at the front quietly weeping. "What are you doing here?" I asked. "I'm responding to your word," she replied. I was shocked as she told her story. She said, "It's not a migraine, it's from brain damage. I was an emergency birth and I stopped breathing as they got me out. They managed to resuscitate me but in the moments before I began to breathe there was some brain damage. The main way it shows itself is severe headaches on the left hand side."

Then she began to sob as she said, "The thing is, my twin sister didn't make it. She died in the womb and I survived. For twenty-seven years I have felt so guilty that I lived and she died. I keep thinking, 'the wrong sister survived.'"

God wanted to speak to her so we could pray into the pain she'd been holding on to for all of those years. I don't know if her headaches went, but I know the Lord miraculously told her that she shouldn't feel guilty about being alive. Her heart was healed in that moment. God knew that if I had time to think about the last part of the prophecy I could well have chickened-out of saying it, so he popped the thought into my head and I found myself saying it before I could think.

YOU HEAR IT

Sometimes "hearing God speak" is not the most helpful phrase. It could cause us to expect to hear a deep booming voice from a cloud. Though God does sometimes speak audibly, this is rare. Even in Acts most of the conversations between the apostles and God happen within a vision (Acts 10:9–15; 18:9–10; 22:17–21). In Paul's account of his encounter with Jesus on the road to Damascus he recalls, "My companions saw the light, but they did not understand the voice of him who was speaking to me" (Acts 22:9). This implies that it wasn't an audible voice that a room of people might understand—it was something that Paul, Peter or others heard internally.

As we've seen, revelation can come in any number of ways. Just as we can "see" something on the screen of our mind, so too there is a form of inner "hearing". The most straightforward way we can describe this is that a thought comes into your mind that isn't your thought.

Mike

This is the main way that God will speak to me. On the same evening I had the words of "Dancing Queen" going through my head, I had an even stranger word. A woman came forward to be prayed for and immediately the word *skubala* entered my head. This is the Greek word for excrement. I had spoken to this woman earlier in the evening and I knew she'd spent time in Greece but I didn't know anything else about her. I remember thinking, *There is absolutely no way I am saying that!* My plan was when my friend Bruce turned to me I would just say, "Pass."

Unfortunately, Bruce turned to me and to my horror said, "Mike, I think God's just told me that he's given you a word for this woman." I couldn't believe it! I decided to go for it, took a deep breath and applied the word as best I could, saying, "Please forgive me, but I think the Lord wants to say to you that in his eyes, you are not a *skubala*." To my amazement the woman broke down in tears. She was sobbing inconsolably for about half an hour. When she recovered a little she told us her story.

She had been married to a Greek and had moved to live with him. He had treated her terribly. One of the ways he had abused her is he would never call her by her name, he would always use the word *skubala*. When they had people round he would say, "*Skubala,* get the drinks." When they went to parties he would introduce her by saying, "This is my *skubala*." For that woman to hear those words from God restored and healed her—it strengthened, encouraged and comforted her in the most miraculous of ways. I had no idea. Looking back, it scares me how close I came to not sharing the word—what a blessing we both would have missed.

YOU KNOW IT

Having said that we can see, feel, speak and hear God's voice, sometimes it is none of the above. Sometimes you might just have a sudden conviction about something—you don't know how you know it, you just know that you do. Jesus was given revelations about the Samaritan woman (John 4:18, 19, 29); the presence of money inside a fish (always useful) (Matt. 17:27); and about a kind of demon that was troubling a boy (Mark 9:17, 25).

Sometimes this "knowing" involves a "double take". You catch someone out of the corner of your eye without meaning to, and you look again. You have a sense that for some reason you are meant to pray for them. Of course, this could just be a natural response if, say for example, they are wearing a Chelsea shirt and you feel an urge to cast something out of them. But we need to learn that at times this might be God and act accordingly.

This seems to be what happened in Acts 3. Peter and John were heading to the temple and passed a lame beggar. There would have been lots of beggars around, but something about this particular guy, on this particular day caused the disciples to do a double take. When the beggar called to them, "Peter looked intently at him, as did John, and said,

'Look at us.'" (Acts 3:4 NRSV). Peter must have somehow known God was at work. Without thinking twice, he said, "'Silver or gold I do not have, but what I do have I give you. In the name of Jesus Christ of Nazareth, walk.' Taking him by the right hand, he helped him up, and instantly the man's feet and ankles became strong" (vv. 3:6–7).

We get other indications of Peter's sudden confidence of God's revelation when he challenged Ananias and Sapphira for attempting to lie to the Holy Spirit (Acts 5:1–10). They both ended up dead. Hopefully this won't happen the first time you take a risk with a prophecy …

These "knowings" may well be the gift of faith (1 Cor. 12:9) that gives a supernatural surge of confidence. The best way we can describe it is that for some reason, without being clear on how you know, you just know that you do. To put it another way, you know it in your "knower".

Andy

One time I was leading the evening service at church and when we made space for the Holy Spirit to meet people about twenty people were being prayed for. I noticed one young lady who had come forward for prayer. She received prayer for about five minutes, thanked the person who was praying and went and sat down. This doesn't happen to me very often but I knew God wasn't finished. I had a strong conviction that God wanted to break something off her.

I went up to her and said, "I'm so sorry, I know you've had prayer but I think there might be some more God wants to do. Would you mind if we prayed with you a bit more?"

As we sat to pray, this lady told my colleague and myself that she had crippling anxiety about her future. She hadn't been an anxious person but it had been a real battle for the last year and she found herself paralysed by indecision. Her words to us were, "I felt the anxiety begin to lift when I was being prayed for, but then when I sat down and started talking to my friend I could feel it creeping back. I thought, 'It hasn't gone after all.'"

We prayed for her to be filled with the Holy Spirit, and God met with her in a powerful way. I was hugely encouraged, and as I walked home that night I thought, *God, you do speak to me*, and, *I must step out next time I find myself with a conviction I can't explain.*

What we are trying to say is that God can speak in any number of ways. They are normal and everyday ways that often don't feel particularly spiritual or significant. A key part of moving in the prophetic is learning to discern when the Lord is speaking. Sometimes it might just be us or something dodgy that we've eaten, but you'll be amazed as you begin to step out how much God wants to speak to you and through you.

GUIDANCE FOR PROPHETS WITH "L-PLATES"

We've looked at three steps that are important as you begin to practise prophecy: know why prophecy is given, understand what the process might look like and start to recognise the everyday, gentle ways that God speaks to us. Here are a few final tips if you'd like to grow in this gift:

HOW TO TEST A PROPHECY

"How do you know if it's God or if it's you?" This is probably the most commonly asked question when it comes to hearing God. The answer is simple: you don't. The only thing you can do is share the prophecy and find out afterwards. Even the apostle Paul wrote, "For we know in part and we prophesy in part" (1 Cor. 13:9). The more we do this the more we grow in discernment, but no one ever gets to a place where God removes the need for trusting him and taking a risk. Nor does anyone get to a place where they never mishear God.

Having said that, there are some tests we can apply to a prophecy:

1. **Does it contradict the Bible?** If we give, or are given, a prophecy that contradicts the Bible the prophecy is wrong. There are no exceptions to this.
2. **Does it strengthen, encourage and comfort?**

Mike

When I started travelling for work, I had a terrible phobia of flying and once before a trip someone came up to me and said, "The Lord wants to say to you, 'Your plane will crash and you will die.'" Needless to say, this did not strengthen, encourage or comfort me! Thankfully I knew enough to know this wasn't how God would speak to me, so I went on the flight and everything was fine.

3. **Do others affirm the prophecy?** 1 Corinthians 14:29 tells us that "Two or three prophets should speak, and the others should weigh carefully what is said." Sometimes it's important to consider with others in the church family whether a prophecy is from God. Most of what Paul writes about spiritual gifts in Corinthians is for the context of the gathered church.

HOW TO SHARE A PROPHECY

The best way to share a prophecy is humbly and kindly. We need to be pastoral as well as prophetic. It's important to recognise when giving any prophecy that (a) we could be wrong, and (b) we could be right and the person might not be willing to receive it yet. Sometimes we have to give people time to digest what the Lord is saying.

Our advice is that rather than strolling up to someone and yelling, "THUS SAITH THE LORD ..." we recognise our limitations and instead begin with something like, "I could be wrong, but I wonder if the Lord is saying ..." If they look blankly at you, or say, "No, I don't think that's right," then don't push it. Our responsibility is to give the prophecy with humility and love, it is not our responsibility how others receive it.

HOW TO GROW IN PROPHECY

It is worth repeating that the best place from which to prophesy is an intimate relationship with the Lord. The more you know who he is the more you will be able to discern whether it is him who is speaking. Let your priority be to seek him before seeking prophecy and you will find prophecy becomes more frequent along the way.

Paul writes in Romans 12:6 that we should "prophesy in accordance with [our] faith." We have noticed that when we step out in the faith that we have, that faith grows. Reading a book will only get you so far. The best way to build your prophecy muscle is to exercise it. If you say it humbly and lovingly but get it wrong, nobody dies, and you learn a lesson. If it's the Lord, someone gets blessed. Most of us have tended to err on the side of silence unless we're sure. If we followed that principle none of us would ever say anything! By stepping out humbly and in love we have nothing to lose and everything to gain.

The best way to grow in prophecy is to get out there and practise it. Go and find a victim.

9

PRAYING FOR HEALING

When Jesus had called the Twelve together, he gave them power and
authority to drive out all demons and to cure diseases, and he sent
them out to proclaim the kingdom of God and to heal the sick.

Luke 9:1–2

In April 2015 Mike was visiting our friends at LIV Village near Durban in South Africa. LIV is an amazing home for orphans and vulnerable children which was founded and led by a wonderful couple called Tich and Joan Smith. Mike was introduced to Ann, the senior social worker at the village. Let your faith be uplifted as you read about Ann's experience …

ANN'S STORY

Ann was losing her eyesight and the doctors in South Africa had said there was nothing more they could do; soon she would be completely blind. Her final hope was visiting the UK to see a consultant at Moorfields Eye Hospital that August, but disappointingly the consultant at Moorfields confirmed the prognosis of the South African doctors.

Before flying home, Ann was persuaded by Tich and Joan to join them for two days at our Soul Survivor summer conference. Whilst she was with us some of the young people prayed for her and to everyone's amazement and joy her eyesight improved significantly. She could see colours again and was able to climb stairs unassisted. Six months later Ann's eyes have maintained the improvement and there has been no further deterioration. She is not 100 per cent healed, but she is certainly not blind as the doctors were expecting her to be by now.

The two of us have never seen someone with such a severe eye condition improve when we have prayed. A bunch of teenagers, who do not have our qualifications, our theological understanding, our spiritual and emotional maturity, prayed for her and saw a minor miracle. Both of us wanted to gather these upstarts and question their theological credentials. Unfortunately, by the time we arrived they'd wandered off.

This is how it should be! These young people prayed with faith and expectation (they didn't know any better) and God moved.

ADVANCING THE KINGDOM

As Jesus began his ministry he stood up in a synagogue in Nazareth and read from the prophet Isaiah,

> The Spirit of the Lord is on me,
>   because he has anointed me
>   to proclaim good news to the poor.
> He has sent me to proclaim freedom for the
>   prisoners
>   and recovery of sight for the blind,

> to set the oppressed free,
>   to proclaim the year of the Lord's favour.
>   (Luke 4:18–19)

He then spent the next three years proclaiming the coming of the kingdom of God in both his teaching and his actions. He preached good news to the poor and he healed the eyes of the blind. Everywhere he went he was good news. Lepers were cleansed, the lame could walk, the demonically oppressed were set free and even the dead were raised. Why did he do this? There were two reasons. The first is because he had compassion for those who were broken physically, emotionally and spiritually. He healed because he loved.

The second reason is that he came to announce the coming of the kingdom of God. What will this future kingdom look like? Everyone will live in a relationship of love and obedience to King Jesus and in relationships of love and mutual submission and service to one another. In God's kingdom no one will be hungry, no one will be oppressed and there will be no injustice. Everyone will be well spiritually, emotionally, mentally and physically. To quote Revelation 21:4, "He will wipe every tear from their eyes. There will be no more death or mourning or crying or pain …" When Jesus came to earth he not only announced this kingdom, he also demonstrated what it would look like. So he called people into relationship with himself (evangelism), into relationship with each other (fellowship) and into wholeness (healing of the body and the heart).

He gave his disciples the same ministry. He told them to go into all the world proclaiming the coming of the kingdom by preaching the gospel, building the community called the church and healing the sick (see Matt. 10:7–8, Luke 9:1–6 and Acts 1:8). We read how the first Christians did this in the Acts of the Apostles. They preached the gospel, they shared their possessions, they gave to the poor, they healed the sick and the church grew (Acts 2:42–47).

Jesus calls us to the exact same ministry! He even tells us to pray, "Your kingdom come, your will be done, on earth as it is in heaven" (Matt. 6:10). We pray that the love, joy and peace of heaven comes down to earth. This includes healing. Can we expect the kingdom to come completely and perfectly? Yes. When Jesus returns everything will be put right. In the meantime, through our obedience, faith, prayer and proclamation, we can expect the coming kingdom of God to break into the present.

There should be signs of the kingdom advancing now. Every time we preach the gospel and someone finds salvation in Jesus, the kingdom advances. Every time relationships are restored and the new community of the church is built, the kingdom advances. Every time the hungry are fed and the homeless are given shelter in his name, the kingdom advances. Every time someone is healed in heart, soul or body, the kingdom advances. Will everyone we proclaim the gospel to give their lives to Jesus? No. Will every relationship be restored this side of heaven? No. Will every injustice be overcome? Not yet. Will everyone we pray for be healed? Not until he returns. However, we don't stop preaching the gospel, building community, fighting for justice or praying for the sick. We believe that we are called to usher in more and more of the kingdom of the future into the present.

This is *why* we pray for healing but *how* should we pray for healing? The following is not an exhaustive answer to this question, more a sharing of some lessons we and our friends have learnt along the way.

FOUR VALUES OF HEALING MINISTRY

We will begin with four biblical values which should form the basis for anything we do for Jesus.

1. WE VALUE THE CROSS

How does valuing the work of Jesus on the cross affect the way we pray for healing? It means we understand that our confidence in asking for healing rests not on how good we are but on how good Jesus is. Our trust is not based on what we do but on what he has done. When Jesus said on the cross, "It is finished" (John 19:30), he meant just that. We are made completely right with God by Jesus's death in our place. We don't earn healing by our goodness, enthusiasm or work any more than we earn forgiveness. Rather, "By *his* wounds *we* are healed" (Isa. 53:5).

Mike insisted that the following illustrations were put in; Andy objected. Mike included them anyway.

If Mike compares himself to Andy, he can be quite pleased with himself. He is taller, better looking, funnier and more substantial. He could easily persuade himself that he is better qualified to pray for healing. However, at the foot of the cross, Andy and Mike are the same. When our qualification comes from Jesus we are *all* qualified. In truth, most of us don't compare ourselves with others and feel better, we compare and feel worse. When we look at the cross we realise it's not about our strengths or our weaknesses, our successes or our failures. It is about Jesus and the victory he won at Calvary.

In the same way, if we value the work of Jesus on the cross, we will never pray like this: "Lord, bless and heal Laura because she has been so good and faithful and she really deserves it." For every Laura there will also be an Andy (see what we did there?), who we are quite sure has been obnoxious and really doesn't deserve it. The truth is that none of us deserve anything. Our prayer should rather be: "Lord, bless and heal Laura and Andy because you are a wonderful Saviour and on the cross you were wounded for our healing." No one "earns" healing any more than anyone can "earn" salvation. Jesus paid the price so we wouldn't have to.

If we value the work of Jesus on the cross we will also understand that the ultimate healing is to know and receive the forgiveness of our sins and the restoration of relationship with God. This is why, whilst we should rejoice if someone's knee is better, it is nothing compared to the rejoicing in heaven and on earth when someone finds salvation in Jesus.

2. WE VALUE THE BIBLE

The Bible is the word of God. The Scriptures must be our ultimate authority in all matters of faith (what we believe) and conduct (how we behave). This means we will seek to make sure that our practice is in line with biblical principles.

Sometimes we hear stories of Christians doing strange things in other parts of the world and people being healed or set free. We can then focus on the strange practices rather than the healing. Our first question as followers of Jesus shouldn't be "Does it work?" but "Is it biblical?"

One of our spiritual heroes is a man called Smith Wigglesworth. He lived in the first half of the last century and had no formal education. He was known as "The Apostle of Faith" and there are many stories of miracles that happened around him. On one occasion he was asked to pray for a man who had terminal stomach cancer. As Smith prayed for the cancer to leave he got very excited. In order to help the cancer on its way, he punched the man in the stomach! The man fell to the ground. The amazing thing is he then got up healed (though we suspect he may have had bruising from the punch).

When we first heard this story we became quite enthusiastic; there are a few people we would enjoy praying for like that! It gives a new definition to the term "the laying on of hands". Then we wondered, "Why *can't* we sometimes pray for people like this? Wigglesworth did it and the man was healed. That must mean it's okay to punch people when you are praying for them." But just because something worked once doesn't mean we should put our trust in it and make it our go-to move. Wigglesworth is one of our spiritual heroes, but Jesus is our model for ministry. There's no record in Scripture of Jesus punching people to heal them.

At the same time, we don't want to turn the Bible into a medical text book. We are trying to discern the *general principles* of Scripture. For example, if we are about to pray for someone who is blind we could go to the gospels with the question "How did Jesus do it?" On one occasion Jesus commanded sight to come (Luke 18:35–43). On another occasion he spat on the ground, made a paste and put it in a man's eyes (John 9:1–12). On a third occasion he didn't even bother with the paste, he spat directly in a person's eye (Mark 8:22–26). In this instance the person had a partial healing and said, "I can see people like trees moving." (This may have been because his eyes were covered with Jesus's saliva.) Jesus placed his hands over the man's eyes and his sight was completely restored. How do we know when to speak and when to spit? Also, what if someone with a bad knee comes to us? Then we're stuck—there's no record of how Jesus healed a knee.

The Bible isn't meant to be a step-by-step guide to praying for various conditions; we look to it for principles not techniques. One principle is that Jesus always seemed to treat people kindly. Punching them doesn't fall into that category.

3. WE VALUE THE LEADING OF THE SPIRIT

We love the way the Nicene Creed describes the Holy Spirit as "The Lord, the giver of life." Healing is his work, not ours. It is the Spirit who gives life, and as Lord, it is the Spirit who gives direction.

The whole of Jesus's earthly ministry was carried out in the power of the Spirit. Jesus clearly looked to his Father for direction as to what he should be doing. In John 5:1–15 he approached one of many crippled beggars at the pool of Bethesda. The beggar had been a cripple for thirty-eight years and on this occasion he was the only person Jesus healed. Later, when explaining himself to the Pharisees, Jesus said, "Very truly I tell you, the Son can do nothing by himself; he can do only *what he sees his Father doing*, because whatever the Father does the Son also does" (John 5:19). We need to learn to wait for the Spirit, to listen to the Spirit and to cooperate with the Spirit so that we can see what the Father is doing.

Of course, we should be open to praying for anyone who asks for healing. Jesus healed everyone who came to him. However, our prayers will be more effective as we learn to discern what the Father is doing and join in. There will also be some people who will never ask for prayer and the Father, by his Spirit, may whisper to us, "Go pray for them, I want to heal them." Both of us have wasted too much of our lives telling God what we wanted to do and asking him to bless it. We have discovered that it's so much more fun and effective finding out what he's doing and joining in with that.

4. WE VALUE THE DIGNITY OF EACH PERSON

Jesus said, "Feed my sheep," not, "Try experiments on my rats."[1] Jesus's motive when praying for people was compassion (Matt. 9:36; 14:14). People we pray for are not objects, but each one is a person made in the image of God (Gen. 1:27). Jesus's new commandment was, "As I have loved you, so you must love one another" (John 13:34). We are to treat each human being with love, gentleness and respect. This means honouring them as valuable and valued in the sight of God. So we never suggest they haven't been healed because of a lack of faith, or insist that they will always have stomach problems until they can forgive their brother. We remind them of how God sees them and how much he cares as we pray. When we have finished praying for someone, whether they are healed or not, they should always leave with a sense of both God's love and ours.

DIFFERENT TYPES OF HEALING

There are different types of hurt and so of course there can be different types of healing. God can heal broken lives and broken hearts as well as broken bodies. It is part of God's character to heal; he said to the Israelites, "I am the LORD, who heals you" (Exod. 15:26). When he came as Jesus to save us he came to draw us into wholeness. In fact, the Greek which means "I save" also means "I heal".[2] It might be helpful to distinguish between four types of healing and look at how they relate to one another.

1. PHYSICAL HEALING

Jesus healed people's bodies two thousand years ago and he continues to do so through his church today. Sickness, disease and death are not sent from God, they are the works of the devil that came into the world when Adam and Eve walked away from God, the source of life and wholeness. Jesus came to restore that which was lost. As he had compassion on those with broken bodies when he walked the earth, he continues to have the same compassion for those who suffer physically today.

Andy

I've been a little tough to convince when it comes to believing God heals today. I think it's a reflection of the fact that I can be naturally quite sceptical and miracles, by their nature, are hard to believe in. Over the years, however, I've come to understand the power of God to heal. This has partly been through increased trust in God's promises; it's also been because I've seen it all around me. Two stories that stand out in my mind are from Soul Survivor events and occurred when the young people were praying for each other.

One young man with a cast on his leg approached me and told me he had broken his ankle just two days before. He had an X-ray at the local hospital, was told the ankle was broken and then his foot and lower leg had been put in a cast. After being prayed for he told me he could feel no pain when he put his weight on the foot and that he'd been completely healed! I was thrilled for him but said, "Just to be sure, leave the cast on and go and see a doctor before you do anything." This young man went away and completely ignored my advice. He took his cast off. He came up waving it at me that night, hopping around on his healed foot! I guess he knew what he was doing after all.

Last summer a young lady came up to me during one of the meetings, incredibly excited. She told me that her friends had been praying for her jaw and it had just been miraculously healed. She explained that for two years she hadn't been able to open her jaw more than a centimetre, and she had been due to have another operation on it in a few months' time. I could see from the way she was speaking that her mouth now seemed totally normal. Eating had of course been hard for her when she could barely open her mouth and she said, "One of the first things I'm going to do is go and take a great big bite of a burger!" Later the same day she came back with her mum to show me pictures on her phone of her eating that burger; both of them were totally delighted!

2. EMOTIONAL HEALING

All of us are emotionally broken in some way, it is the inevitable consequence of living in a broken world. Emotional and mental illness is rampant in our society and many of us struggle with a lack of significance or self-worth. Many are brokenhearted and live lives of screaming emotional agony or quiet desperation. Self-harm, addiction, chronic anxiety and depression are huge issues for our generation. Jesus comes to bring us salvation in every sense of the word. He not only desires to heal our broken bodies, he wants to also heal our broken hearts.

In Jesus's presence the pain we carry, the secret shame we bear, begins to be released. This can seem quite messy and frightening for a while. As pain is released in the presence of Jesus and by the power of the Holy Spirit, there can often be many tears and even, at times, cries of agony. There then follows a deep peace as folk are filled with the knowledge of the love of God, and the memories or traumas lose their hold over people's lives. When we pray we are to pray for emotional healing confidently and with expectation but also with gentleness and kindness. We should also take our time and make space for Jesus to encounter someone while we bless what he is doing. There are few things more beautiful to see than people released from pain or shame that has bound them, sometimes for years.

Mike

In 1986 I arrived at St Andrew's, Chorleywood, a very broken person. So many things in my life had gone wrong. My parents had immigrated to England from Cyprus, and when I began school I could speak very little English. I was incredibly shy and my first months at school were sheer agony. I couldn't communicate with the other kids and I used to wander round the playground on my own while everyone played together around me. After a while I started to hide in the toilet or behind a wall during break times so no one would see my shame. I felt different; the brown foreigner.

In time the other kids began to include me in their games, but the feeling of being the outsider lingered for years. This feeling became so overpowering that for a while in my early teens I found it easier to withdraw into my own safe, if lonely, world than go through the exhaustion and pain of maintaining relationships. I would go silent on people and at times completely shut down. My twenties were fairly miserable as everything I tried to do seemed to go wrong. Whenever there was any conflict or an awkward situation in a relationship I would find myself retreating into silence. Silence was my safe place.

Then I heard about this church that prayed for people for healing. One afternoon, in my desperation, I caught the train to Chorleywood and went to the evening service. Immediately I knew I had come home. Waves of love swept over me. Little did I know that in a couple of years I would become the full-time youth pastor there and go on to plant Soul Survivor Watford and begin Soul Survivor ministries too.

The vicar of the church, David Pytches, and his wife Mary for some inexplicable reason took an interest in me and encouraged me, challenged me, made time for me and basically loved me. When they discovered that I was a man in pain, Mary and another saint, Prue Bedwell, met with me every Friday for over two years to talk with me and pray for my heart to be healed and set free. I have no idea where I would be if God had not put these people in my life but I shudder at the thought. My healing has been a process and I know that I shall walk into heaven with a limp, but because of the power of God and the love and prayers of his people I discovered amazing healing.

3. DELIVERANCE FROM DEMONIC OPPRESSION

Sometimes when people have suffered severe physical or emotional trauma or when they have become addicted to a sinful and destructive habit, they can be affected by demonic oppression. By this we do not mean they are "possessed" by demons; that is quite rare. We mean that a demon can attach itself to an aspect of a person's life and keep them bound to an addiction or destructive behaviour. In Ephesians 4:27 Paul warns us against giving the devil a "foothold". Sometimes by immersing ourselves in certain behaviours we are giving the devil an open door into affecting our minds or hearts.

Deliverance is sometimes necessary to set a person free to receive physical or emotional healing. If we think there may be demonic activity in an area of a person's life who we are praying for, we don't need to get excited. We don't need to get the stake or the garlic out; it's only a little demon. Jesus broke the power of Satan and his entourage on the cross. All we have to do is quietly command the demon to leave in the name of Jesus and it will. Jesus has not only made the power of the Holy Spirit available to us, he has also given us authority. Often the person we are praying for doesn't even need to know that we are casting out a demon. We often say something like: "If there is any spirit here contrary to the Spirit of Jesus, you must leave now." That usually does the trick!

4. SPIRITUAL HEALING

The greatest healing is, of course, conversion. The ultimate healing is to be reconciled with God and to know and receive his forgiveness and cleansing. Linked to this is to come to a place of reconciliation with others and to give and receive forgiveness and this often results in releasing physical and emotional healing. We are amazed at the number of people who are healed emotionally or physically once they have received forgiveness from God and released forgiveness to someone who has hurt them.

We finish this overview of the types of healing ministry with these words from James:

> Is anyone among you ill? Let them call the elders of the church to pray over them and anoint them with oil in the name of the Lord. And the prayer offered in faith will make the sick person well; the Lord will raise them up. If they have sinned, they will be forgiven. Therefore confess your sins to each other and pray for each other so that you may be healed. The prayer of a righteous person is powerful and effective. (James 5:14–16)

It's key to note the command to pray for the sick, James's confidence that the prayers will be answered, the central place of spiritual healing ("If they have sinned they will be forgiven") and finally the importance of having right relationships with one another ("confess your sins to each other and pray for each other so that you may be healed").

NOTHING TO LOSE

It can be tempting to pray for healing only when we are full of expectancy or when we think we'll see a "result", but, like Jesus, our motivation should be compassion not success. Once when Jesus was looking for somewhere to rest on the shores of Lake Galilee a crowd of people arrived ahead of him. We read in Matthew 14:14, "When Jesus landed and saw a large crowd, he had compassion on them and healed those who were ill." When our motivation is that people will see the goodness, mercy and compassion of God, we will pray regardless of likely "success". Even if the person isn't healed they will still almost always feel loved and cared for.

One of the most painful losses we've known in the last few years was the death of our friend Bob. Bob was the associate pastor of our church; he was an incredibly close friend and a father figure to many in our church family. In 2011 Bob was diagnosed with stomach cancer—a particularly aggressive type of cancer. He was told he would need to undergo serious treatment, but that his chances of survival were very low.

We'll never forget the service when this was announced to the church. People were shocked and many wept. As one we pushed all the chairs to the side and hundreds of us gathered around Bob and his wife Ruth to pray for healing. We continued to pray persistently and faithfully for Bob throughout his treatment. Eventually he underwent an operation and, against the odds, the cancer was removed. He was given the all-clear by the doctors. Bob was weakened by the ordeal but we rejoiced and celebrated together.

Bob went on to enjoy a good quality of life for quite some time. However, the following year he was rushed to hospital on Boxing Day. The cancer had come back and the doctors said this time there was nothing they could do. Bob was given just a few months to live. Again we grieved together as a church, and again we prayed. Without being asked, a number in the church gave generously in order to enable Bob to fly to Germany for groundbreaking treatment. There were ups and downs along the journey. At times Bob seemed to be making progress, at other points he was a shadow of himself. He lived for almost a year and a half after that terminal diagnosis, but then the Lord took him home. Neither of us will ever forget the effect the cancer had on Bob's body, nor the courage and determination with which he fought it. We miss him dearly.

Although Bob wasn't healed, praying for his healing advanced Jesus's kingdom. He and his family were incredibly grateful for the prayers of their church family. Bob lived far longer than was originally expected—partly because of great medical care, but also partly, he (and we) believed, because of answers to prayer. He and Ruth both said those years were some of the richest of their lives. Our church has many faults (not least the two senior pastors) but if it has a strength it is that we are a loving community. No one among us regrets praying for healing; it is how we show love. When compassion motivates our prayer, at best someone is loved and healed but at worst they are loved.

PRAYING FOR HEALING: AN IDIOT'S GUIDE

Here is a simple model for praying for healing. For the sake of ease we've largely focused on physical healing but it wouldn't be difficult to apply the principles to another type of hurt. This isn't meant to be a straightjacket or a list of rules. We suggest it as a model of prayer that is accessible to anyone.

WHO IS RESPONSIBLE FOR WHAT?

When praying for healing it's helpful to remind ourselves where our responsibility begins and where it ends. We are like waiters and waitresses in a restaurant. We may ask the customer, "What is your order, madam?" She may reply, "I have a bad left knee I would like healed." We can note that down. We may even ask, "How would you like that, madam: rare, medium or well-done?" Then in prayer we take the order to the chef. Only he can cook the meal but we are involved in its delivery. When we understand this it takes away all the pressure and actually makes it much more fun. Sometimes the customer even thanks us for the wonderful meal. It is quite important that as we receive the thanks we remember that we don't deserve it and instead give credit and thanks to the chef. This is called worship! It is our responsibility to ask and pray; it is God's job to heal.

WHERE DOES IT HURT?

When someone approaches us for prayer the first question we ask is, "Where does it hurt?" We know this seems obvious but you would be amazed at the number of people we have seen praying for someone and then when we ask them what they are praying for they have no idea. If they respond by giving you their full medical history, stop them. Most of us are not doctors. If we discover that their condition is horrendous and has been deteriorating for the last twenty years we may feel faith draining out of the soles of our feet. A brief, simple description is all we need in order to pray.

FOLLOW THE LEAD OF THE SPIRIT

At this point we need to be listening to the prompting of the Spirit. What is the Father telling us to do? There are a few different ways we could pray; it's a question of knowing which tool we should use.

- **Speak to the condition.** Jesus often did this. So too did some of the early church—for example, when Peter spoke to the crippled beggar: "Silver or gold I do not have, but what I do have I give you. In the name of Jesus Christ of Nazareth, walk" (Acts 3:6). We don't have any power to heal but all authority in heaven and on earth belongs to Jesus and we are his ambassadors. This means we carry something of his authority; we speak on behalf of the king. Imagine if we walked into the middle of a busy road and held up our hands to stop traffic. We would probably be flattened! If we put on a police uniform and did the same thing the drivers would pay attention. We'd still be just as puny but we'd have authority. Jesus gives us the authority to heal—he commands us to pray in his name (Matt. 10:8; Luke 9:1; John 15:16). When you speak to the condition you speak in the name of the king.
- **Invite the Spirit, then watch and listen.** On other occasions, we invite the presence of the Holy Spirit upon the individual, ask him to guide us, and watch and listen to what the Father is doing and saying.

Often the first indication that the Spirit is at work is that the person we're praying for begins to look peaceful. It can be helpful to gently lay a hand in an appropriate place (a shoulder is usually a safe bet); this was something Jesus did (Luke 4:40). Whilst we are praying and waiting it can also be helpful to be asking the Father for direction. Sometimes you may get a prophetic word or a picture. Often humbly sharing these insights can be helpful. As we mentioned earlier sometimes there seems to be a connection between spiritual and physical healing; asking God to help us discern the cause of the condition can help us know what needs to be prayed into.

The important thing is to wait and to watch. We don't need to hurry. Occasionally when the power of God's presence comes upon an individual there might be what some would call a "power encounter". The person may begin to shake, their eyes may flutter, or there may be other physical responses. We don't need to start hyperventilating when this happens. It is a human response to the presence of God. Sometimes it can seem like electricity coursing through a person's body. Often this is a sign that healing is taking place. We can quietly praise God for what he's doing and pray that the person would be soaked in his presence. (Remember what we focused on in chapter 1: the power is in the presence.)

Sometimes there may be an emotional response. The person may begin to weep or even laugh. While we don't ever want to hype-up emotionalism, neither do we want to be afraid of emotions. Often this can be a sign that God is healing someone's heart. Many of us bury pain in order to survive. Unfortunately, the pain doesn't go away, it simply eats us up inside. When God's love rests on a person, often they instinctively know that they are in a safe place to express the pain, perhaps for the first time.

Mike

Some years ago I met a youth leader at a forum in the south of England. She was twenty-six years old and seemed very much in control. She was organised and efficient, the sort of person who scares the life out of me. The next time I noticed her was on the first night of a Soul Survivor summer conference, someone was praying for her and she began to scream. The following day she began to scream again. This went on for most of the week. I considered asking her to be quiet. When I saw her on the final day I almost didn't recognise her. She was laughing, looking very relaxed and not the uptight young lady I had met six months earlier.

A few months later she came to see me and told me that when she was thirteen, her stepfather came into her room and abused her. She was very frightened and told her mother, but her mother's response was even more frightening. She told her daughter that she didn't believe her and that if she ever repeated the accusation to anyone else she would have to leave home. This frightened thirteen-year-old swallowed all the fear and the pain in order to survive, and began to lead a relatively emotionless life. She told me that on the first night of the conference she sensed God's love in a powerful way and she could feel the tears and the screams of her thirteen-year-old self coming to the surface. She said, "He healed me. And for the first time in thirteen years I feel alive. I laugh from my belly. I am fully human again. Thank you for not stopping me and for allowing the pain to come out."

———————

Sometimes we have no idea about the pain that people are going through and the healing that Jesus is doing, we just have to give space and time for the Holy Spirit to work and for people to respond. Our job is to keep reassuring them that Jesus is with them and that their Father in heaven loves them.

Some may not exhibit any physical or emotional response. That does not mean that God is not at work. We are all built differently. Some of us respond in a more physical way, others in a more emotional way and others in a more intellectual way. One way is not more spiritual than another. Often we have known people who have seemed to respond the least who have had the deepest encounter with God and the greatest healing. Our focus should not be on manifestations but on Jesus.

CHECK IN

We want to make space for the Spirit to meet with the person and so lots of talking isn't necessary. In fact, it is often counterproductive; we aren't going to talk someone into being healed! At the same time, it can be helpful to check in after a while. It's a good idea to pray with our eyes open—this allows us to watch and see whether God is doing anything. It can also be helpful to occasionally ask questions; see if the person's level of pain has reduced, if he or she has been healed or if God is starting to speak about something specific. If the individual hasn't been healed or doesn't have anything to say, there's no need to worry. Just keep praying. Carry on praying until you sense that the Spirit has finished ministering or the person has had enough.

FOLLOW UP

As the time of prayer comes to an end the important thing is that the person knows they are loved. Regardless of whether someone has been healed we need to make sure he or she is valued.

We would suggest you *don't* say, "You haven't been healed? *Really?* The last five people I've prayed for have all been miraculously and completely healed. There are three reasons why people don't get healed: they don't have enough faith, they have secret sin in their lives, or they have a demon. Which are *you?*" Not only is this not true, it means the person who came forward for healing leaves with their original condition and an added burden that we have put on them.

Instead, we need to make sure the person is assured of God's love and feels totally free to come and ask for prayer again at any point. Jesus teaches that persistence in prayer is important (Luke 18:1–8). If it's appropriate, encourage the person to keep seeking prayer and asking for healing.

BEGIN TODAY

This is an amazing gift to grow in. As we begin to pray for people we'll discover that Jesus sets people free in the most powerful of ways. The best way to learn how to be effective in praying for healing is to pray for healing. It's like learning how to cook. We can read all the cookery books that have ever been written and watch hours of cookery shows on TV, but the only way we will learn how to cook is by actually having a go. When it comes to healing, the best way to learn is by doing.

Mike

I have a friend called Blaine Cook who seems to be able to discern the Holy Spirit at work like nobody else I know. I have seen God use him in remarkable ways and he has probably taught me more about moving in the supernatural power of God than anyone else. Some years ago I invited myself to go and stay with him and his family for a few days at his home in California. My friends Matt and Beth Redman came with me. I was determined to discover the "secret ingredient" that resulted in him being so effective in praying for people so I could use the "formula" and move in a more powerful way as well.

It didn't take me long to discover the formula and it was nothing like I expected. The secret was: *if it moved, Blaine laid hands on it.* One day Blaine drove us from Laguna Hills to Anaheim, a journey that took about thirty minutes. After a short time I coughed. "Are you okay?" he asked. "Just a bit of a cough," I replied. Before I knew it, he was steering with one hand and the other hand was on my chest! "I rebuke this cough in Jesus's name!" he said. A little later on, Beth said, "Matt, do you have any aspirin?" "Why do you need an aspirin?" enquired Blaine. "I have a bit of a headache," she said, and before we knew it Blaine had laid his hand on Beth. By the time we had arrived in Anaheim Blaine had prayed for all three of us while driving the car.

I realised that at least part of the secret to Blaine's effectiveness was that he took every opportunity to minister.

———————

The best way to start praying for healing is to find something that moves and ask, "Where does it hurt?" If we pray with the love and compassion of Jesus, the kingdom is always advanced. Let's pray kindly, expectantly and persistently. As Jesus sent the first disciples "to proclaim the kingdom of God and to heal those who were ill" (Luke 9:2), so he sends us.

10

FOR THE SAKE OF THE WORLD

You will receive power when the Holy Spirit comes on you; and you will be my witnesses in Jerusalem, and in all Judea and Samaria, and to the ends of the earth.

Acts 1:8

It's been said that the Spirit comes to the church en route to the world. The Father sent the Son, the Father and the Son sent the Spirit, and now the Father, Son and Spirit are sending us!

Jesus fills us with his Spirit *in order* that we might go and bear witness to him. The everyday supernatural life is one given over to sharing Jesus with others. Everything we've talked about so far—stepping out in weakness, choosing obedience, listening to God, praying for healing—comes into play. We are created and called to do this outside of the church.

DIFFERENT TYPES OF EVANGELISM

It can be helpful to know that when people talk about evangelism they often break it down into different types.

FRIENDSHIP EVANGELISM

This is evangelism that takes place person to person. It happens through one-on-one relationships at school, in the office and in our families. We witness to people with lives that reflect Jesus and with words that point to him. We are faithful friends and neighbours.

PROCLAMATION EVANGELISM

This is evangelism where the simple message of the gospel is declared. It may often be preached in a church or at an evangelistic event of some kind, or indeed any time we tell someone the gospel and the story of salvation.

PERSUASION EVANGELISM

This evangelism focuses more on presenting the evidence for the truth of Jesus's claims. It often accounts for, and attempts to respond to, commonly asked questions about Christianity.

SERVANT EVANGELISM

This is where we choose to be kind and generous and find ways to serve our neighbours and communities. It may consist of random acts of kindness or a group planning and implementing a project that will make a difference in the lives of others.

POWER EVANGELISM

This type of evangelism is based around the supernatural works of the Holy Spirit—signs and wonders that testify to God's goodness, mercy and compassion.

All evangelism, not just power evangelism, requires the supernatural power of God. We need God's transforming Spirit living inside of us if our lives are to reflect Jesus. It is the Holy Spirit who convicts people of sin and who brings revelation of who Jesus is (John 16:8, 14). However, we especially want to focus on the way the everyday supernatural makes a way for people to come to Jesus.

SUPERNATURAL BREAKTHROUGH

People are not saved because of signs or wonders; they don't pass from death to life because of their trust in a prophetic word. It is only trust in Jesus, his death and his resurrection that has the power to save. However, the supernatural can reveal Jesus. In John's gospel supernatural "signs" point to Jesus's glory and *as a consequence* people put their trust in him (see John 2:11; 14:11). John actually summarises his whole gospel with these words: "Jesus performed many other signs in the presence of his disciples, which are not recorded in this book. But these are written *that you may believe* that Jesus is the Messiah, the Son of God, and that by believing you may have life in his name" (John 20:30–31). In other words, John has written down the miracles and supernatural events of Jesus's ministry because he knows they can lead us to faith.

One of our favourite stories of this happening is from John 4:1–42. Jesus and the disciples had been walking along in the heat of the day. They arrived at a well and Jesus sent all the disciples off into the nearby town with his lunch order. On first reading we wondered why he needed to send all of the disciples to pick up lunch. Then we remembered what the disciples were like; it probably would have taken all twelve of them just to find Tesco.

Meanwhile, a Samaritan woman arrived at the well and began to draw water and Jesus struck up a conversation with her by asking for a drink. This was radical for all sorts of reasons; in that culture Jewish men didn't talk to women they didn't know, and Jews didn't talk to Samaritans. Having asked for a drink Jesus suggested that she should really be asking *him* for a drink: "If you knew the gift of God and who it is that asks you for a drink, you would have asked him and he would have given you living water" (v. 10). Up until this stage the woman was still unclear about what was going on. A breakthrough came when Jesus made this comment:

> He told her, "Go, call your husband and come back."
>
> "I have no husband," she replied.
>
> Jesus said to her, *"You are right when you say you have no husband. The fact is, you have had five*

husbands, and the man you now have is not your hus-
band. What you have just said is quite true."

    "Sir," the woman said, "I can see that you are a
prophet." (vv. 16–19)

We love the way Jesus was able to reveal this woman's shameful
past *and* affirm her at the same time. Five husbands was a little more
than the quota allowed—yet Jesus twice affirmed what she said ("What
you have just said is quite true"). It's a master class in using prophecy to
strengthen, encourage and comfort. It's also a master class in how the
everyday supernatural can play a role in evangelism. It's because of this
prophetic word that the woman suddenly began to realise who Jesus
was. She later ran back to her town saying, "Come, see a man *who told
me everything I've ever done.* Could this be the Messiah?" (v. 29). The
town came running (probably because they wanted to know everything she'd ever done …). Many of them eventually put their trust in
Jesus as "the Saviour of the world" (v. 42).

    This total turnaround can be traced back to a single prophetic
word. Jesus was kind, he treated the woman with dignity when
many wouldn't have done so, and he openly told her about himself.
Evangelism needs all these ingredients. Yet in this instance and many
others, it was his moving in the supernatural that was the key step to
someone coming to know him.

Mike

A number of years ago I went with a team of young people to
take part in a mission in a town called Cullompton in Devon. We

wandered round the town during the day, meeting young people and inviting them to our cafe in the evening. There was one group who went by the name "The Wasters Wall Gang". There were about twelve of them and they seemed to spend most of their time hanging around and sitting on a wall in the town. (There wasn't a huge amount to do in Cullompton!) Everyone thought they were wasting their time and therefore their lives, hence their name. They came along to the cafe in the evenings and they seemed to enjoy the band playing, the karaoke and chatting to people.

On the final night I gave a little talk explaining the good news of Jesus. The Wasters Wall Gang started heckling me. The more I tried to speak the more they enjoyed giving a very loud running commentary on my talk. They were jeering and shouting that God didn't exist, we were just deluded. I struggled to concentrate on what I was saying and everyone else struggled to hear me. Eventually I went over to them, desperate for them to meet Jesus but without a clue what to do.

I said to the leader of the gang, "I know Jesus is here by his Spirit and you don't think he exists. Why don't we conduct an experiment? Why don't you let me pray for you that Jesus would meet with you and we will see what happens?" He hesitantly said, "Okay, then," and I immediately thought, *What have I done?* I felt like a modern-day Elijah but without the power. I put my hands on his head and prayed that Jesus would meet him. The rest of the gang started giggling and I longed for the ground to swallow me up. After a while the young man told the others to shut up. Suddenly everything became serious. I asked him what was going on. He told me that he was feeling a warmth and that he felt lighter. I asked him if it was a good feeling and he readily said it was. Hesitantly he said, "It's like I've got this love inside me."

To cut a long story short, that evening he and about half of his gang gave their lives to Jesus. I nearly passed out.

THE *ACTS* OF THE APOSTLES

In many cases it was the supernatural *acts* of the first disciples that led people to faith. When they were hard pressed and threatened with persecution, they prayed to the Lord, "Stretch out your hand to heal and perform signs and wonders through the name of your holy servant Jesus" (Acts 4:30). God answered this prayer and miracles frequently opened people up to hearing the gospel. When Philip arrived in Samaria, for example, we're told, "When the crowds heard Philip and saw the signs he performed, they all paid close attention to what he said" (8:6).

The supernatural didn't simply draw people to God, it was also God's means of directing the church to reach certain people. One night the Lord gave Paul a vision of a man of Macedonia begging him, "Come over to Macedonia and help us." He and his companions at once got ready and headed there (16:9–10).

Something similar happened in the story of Philip and the Ethiopian eunuch (8:26–40). The Lord told Philip to travel down a particular road—from Jerusalem to Gaza. As he walked along he came across an Ethiopian eunuch. The man was an important official who had been to Jerusalem to worship and was on his way home. As he sat in his chariot he was reading the prophet Isaiah:

The Spirit told Philip, "Go to that chariot and stay near it."

Then Philip ran up to the chariot and heard the man reading Isaiah the prophet. "Do you understand what you are reading?" Philip asked.

"'How can I," he said, "unless someone explains it to me?" So he invited Philip to come up and sit with him. (vv. 29–31)

It just so happened that the Ethiopian was reading Isaiah's description of Jesus's death. Starting with that scripture Philip was able to explain the good news to him. Within a short time, the Ethiopian stopped the chariot and had Philip baptise him in some water by the roadside. The Spirit then whisked Philip off and the Ethiopian went on his way rejoicing.

Philip was supernaturally guided to a particular location; he had what some might call a "divine appointment". He was *meant* to meet the Ethiopian eunuch. In order for this to happen, however, he had to be obedient to God's word. To this day the Ethiopian eunuch is considered by some to be the founder of the church in Ethiopia. The breakthrough came because of Philip's willingness to listen to and obey the direction of God. A similar divine appointment took place when Jesus met Zacchaeus (he miraculously knew his name), and the first time he met Nathanael (Luke 19:1–10; John 1:47–51).

The early believers didn't seek miracles *instead of* witnessing in other ways. They were a community that loved each other and gave to everyone who had need. The accounts we have of their speeches show us that they were amazingly effective in proclaiming the gospel and persuading people of the truth of Jesus. However, supernatural events also gave them an edge. Long arguments can usually be avoided if a person is raised from the dead! If we are to be effective in witnessing to Jesus today, it's vital that we learn to move in the everyday supernatural. Just like the first believers we are called to *proclaim* the kingdom and to *demonstrate* the kingdom.

OUR "CREDENTIALS"

We can often feel less than confident when it comes to evangelism. It's so important to understand that God doesn't just send us to be his witnesses, he equips us for the task! Let's just take a moment to look at our credentials.

AUTHORITY

When the President of the United States sends an ambassador oversees they go with the weight and might of the United States behind them. These individuals might not be the president, but as his representatives they carry his authority. They speak and act on behalf of the most powerful nation on earth. They are empowered to sign certain treaties, to hold discussions at the highest level and to forge new relationships on behalf of their nation.

Those who met Jesus were staggered by the authority he carried. They listened to his teaching and were "amazed ... because he taught them as one who had authority ..." (Mark 1:22). Those who saw his miracles "were filled with awe; and they praised God, who had given such authority to man" (Matt. 9:8). It's an astonishing thing to realise that when Jesus sent out the disciples he gave them *his* authority (Luke 10:19; Matt. 10:1). He told them words to the effect of "*Proclaim* my kingdom and *demonstrate* my kingdom" (Luke 10:9). It is hugely significant that as he was about to ascend to heaven Jesus's final command was to *go, under his authority.* The Great Commission reads, "*All authority* in heaven and on earth *has been given to me.* Therefore *go* and make disciples of all nations … And surely I am with you always, to the very end of the age" (Matt. 28:18–20).

As Jesus's ambassadors we are representatives of the King of kings. He sends us out to proclaim and demonstrate his kingdom. However lacking in confidence we may feel, we have the full weight and might of the Lord of heaven behind us. We have been given authority to share the gospel, to heal the sick and to drive out demons. When we are sent in the name of Jesus we carry the authority of Jesus.

A POWERFUL PARTNER

In Acts, Jesus assures the disciples that if they wait in Jerusalem they will receive the Holy Spirit. He specifically says they will receive the Spirit, that they might be his "*witnesses* in Jerusalem, and in all Judea and Samaria, and to the ends of the earth" (Acts 1:8). Jesus sends us, but he does not send us alone. He is coming with us *through* his Spirit. The Spirit isn't simply "power" for witness; he is a *partner* with us in God's mission.

Andy

I was forced to play rugby at school. I was tiny and so not really suited to it. I'd often get steamrolled by the giant forwards (for some reason that reminds me of working with Mike). I can remember many a grim, grey Wednesday afternoon running around on a muddy pitch. When you have the ball in rugby and see huge opposing players running towards you, one of the most comforting things you can hear are the words "With you!" Someone else on your team is letting you know that you are not alone and they are close by. Whenever I heard the shout "With you!" my tactic was generally to pass the ball onto them and hope they could do more with it than I could.

When we step out to witness for Jesus we don't go alone; we have a powerful partner in the Holy Spirit. It's as if every time we step out he shouts, "With you!" He was beside the apostles when they took risks and he is beside us as well. His overwhelming desire is that Jesus is glorified through us. If we found we had the New Zealand rugby team backing us up we'd feel far more confident on the pitch even with no skill of our own. Likewise, our hope is not that *we* are amazing evangelists, it's that we have the help of the Holy Spirit, the ultimate evangelist. Words like *mission, witness* and *advancing the kingdom* all apply to the supernatural life because they describe the heart of the Spirit. God has put his treasure in our clay jars; we have been empowered.

HOW TO BEGIN

Knowing that we are sent with the authority of Jesus and in the power of the Spirit means we step out with a little more confidence.

How do we begin to witness through the everyday supernatural? What should this look like?

STORIES OF A FAILED "POWER EVANGELIST"

Andy

I have heard many stories about power evangelism. Lots of them have involved very outgoing people praying for complete strangers. They tended to go something along the lines of: "I got on a plane. I chatted to the person next to me. They had a back condition. I prayed for them and it was miraculously healed. They became a Christian." Other stories might include walking up to strangers in the street and giving them incredibly accurate prophetic words. It sounded like something I should be doing!

I've gathered my courage and "gone for it" several times over the years. I remember once being at Belfast airport and thinking it seemed like the right sort of place to have prophetic words for people. A middle-aged lady several steps in front of me in the security queue caught my attention. I ended up following her around the airport for the next fifteen minutes, trying to pluck up the courage to approach her. Eventually, I steeled myself, went up to her and said, "Excuse me, I'm a Christian and I'd like to say to you that Jesus loves you." It was more a blessed thought than an incisive, cutting-to-the-heart prophetic word. Unfortunately, she didn't seem that blessed by it. She just looked embarrassed. To my shame, I felt so awkward I then just walked off without saying anything else! Luckily, she wasn't on my flight.

Another time I was on the train heading into London. It was a busy train but I thought the Lord gave me a message for the person sitting opposite me. Again the message was, "The Lord says, 'I love you and I'll never leave you.'" I couldn't bring myself to share it where everyone could hear so when we arrived at Euston station I followed the person along the platform. (I may have the spiritual gift of following people in public spaces.) I grabbed them just as they were heading through the ticket barrier and delivered my message. Again, they seemed more uncomfortable than anything else. It was another discouraging response. After a few more disappointing attempts, I lost hope and gave up.

A short time ago I heard about an occasion when John Wimber went into the shopping mall and invited the Holy Spirit to come. After a few minutes the Holy Spirit began to move on a lady nearby. She started crying. Wimber went up to her, explained about Jesus and prayed for her. That sounded more manageable to me! I headed to my local shopping centre, found a bench and invited the Holy Spirit to come and meet people. I sat there for two hours waiting for someone to start crying. Nobody did. I gave up and walked home depressed.

RIGHT HEART, DIFFERENT APPROACH

As you might imagine, I felt discouraged by my lack of success in this area. I knew the importance of perseverance—we'll talk about that in the next chapter—so I began to ask questions of people who I knew were moving in these things.

I chatted to someone I knew was amazingly bold in praying for strangers, the type of person who has plenty of "plane stories". I said, "The truth is I'm terrified of doing this a lot of the time. Have you got any advice?" He said, "Yes, you need to throw yourself under a bus!" By this he meant, I was to go out and fail spectacularly (either that or he just didn't like me ...). The theory was that when I failed I would realise it wasn't that bad and I would try again. I pondered his suggestion.

The next day I was talking to someone else (a trained psychologist who was speaking at Soul Survivor) and mentioned the advice I received. This person looked at me kindly and said, "Andy, I'm not sure this is the best approach for you. If you (with your fear of failure) go out and spectacularly fail, you won't just pick yourself up and try again tomorrow. You'll be totally gutted. The most likely response you'll have is, 'I'm *never* doing that again.' You might have another go but it'll take years." His advice to me instead was to begin to work my way up in increments. It's some of the wisest advice I've ever been given in how to begin to move in everyday supernatural evangelism: grow into it.

START IN RELATIONSHIP

One of the main stumbling blocks to power evangelism is that, at the beginning, we make it too hard for ourselves. We divorce it from the other types of evangelism and so we think we're only really doing power evangelism if we are regularly approaching strangers in shops. Instead, power evangelism should *infuse* all our proclamation, persuasion and personal evangelism. Let us be clear: approaching people we have never met with words from God is *part* of this. It's an important part. We've already talked of how Jesus was able to do this, Philip did this, and we know many people who have seen fantastic things happen by stepping out in this way. We both want to grow into doing this more! However, it is only part of what it means to witness in the supernatural power of the Spirit.

The main place this begins for most of us is in the context of the relationships we already have. Before we rush off to find some strangers to pray for let's ask ourselves whether we're praying for our non-Christian family, friends and neighbours. When they were last sick did we ask if we could pray for healing and lay hands on them? When they were stressed did we ask God for a word that would strengthen, encourage and comfort them? Are we even regularly praying for each other in our churches? As one of our friends often says, "The meeting place is the learning place for the market place." If we aren't consistently praying for each other in church we're unlikely to be able to pray for people in the pub.

For most of us praying for total strangers is going to be a challenge. The two of us certainly find it difficult! If, however, we are regularly praying for people that we know, and then we happen to have a conversation with a stranger who tells us they are ill, we will be far better prepared to step out.

Andy

Learning that I should begin to step out in the relationships I already had was a revelation for me. A few weeks ago someone cancelled a meeting because they were ill, so I called and prayed for them over the phone. I didn't know the person well and even though they were a Christian, I was a bit embarrassed, but they said they were very touched that I'd thought to do that. The other day I was walking home and bumped into a guy who lives two doors away from me. He's a removal man and he told me he'd damaged his hand. I asked if I could pray for it. I quickly laid a hand on his wrist, spoke to the condition, and then we carried on chatting normally. He couldn't tell if there had been an improvement right then but I'm planning on asking next time I see him. I've already grown in confidence in stepping out in this way.

EVERYDAY EXPECTATION

Whenever we've come across people who seem to be moving in the everyday supernatural we have tried to find out their secret. One friend of ours seems to have prophetic words for every other person he meets. He has spoken powerfully into both of our lives and is an incredibly effective evangelist. He is a businessman; during several years at one company he personally led over four hundred of the employees to Jesus. It sounds almost unbelievable but we have seen him in action. He is kind, he cares deeply about people, and he trusts the Holy Spirit to guide him. It's not unusual for him to start prophesying to the person he sits next to in a restaurant or meets in the street.

Once when chatting over lunch, we asked the question that had been bothering us for a while, "Why does God seem to use you to do all these things but he doesn't seem to use us?" "Why does God use me?" He paused, thinking for a moment, and then replied, "It's because I have a high expectation that God will use me. You don't. God loves people. He wants to bless them. I am available for him to use me. Why wouldn't he want to?" It was both simple and profound. Our friend is certainly gifted but it is this *expectation* that God will use him because he wants to bless people that shapes his day.

How would our approach to things change if we had a confident expectation that God would use us? We have the authority and we have the power. We know God *wants* to reach his world. We know it's not about our strength but about God operating through us. What's more, in Ephesians 2:10 Paul writes, "For we are God's handiwork, created in Christ Jesus to do good works, which God prepared in advance for us to do." In other words, each day there are people God *prepared* for us to bless. Our job is to be attentive, listen to the Spirit, and get ready to step out. We've talked about how Jesus paid close attention to what his Father was doing and said, "I only do what I see my Father doing." In the same conversation he also said, "My Father is always at his work ..." (John 5:17). We only do what we see our Father doing, but our Father is *always* doing something! As we approach the day with expectation, we'll begin to pick up on the God-opportunities all around us.

EVERYDAY OPPORTUNITIES

When we do find ourselves praying for people who aren't Christians, whether strangers or friends, we usually don't have much time. They aren't used to being prayed for or waiting on the Spirit. They'll often have their eyes open and stare at you when you pray!

If you are offering to pray for someone it might be helpful to say something like, "I'm a Christian, would you mind if I prayed for you?" Then pray a brief prayer; if you are praying for healing it might help to lay a hand on them (with their permission). Afterwards, it can be helpful to say, "Thank you so much for letting me have a go!" and to assure them of Jesus's love. They are usually not expecting anything to happen and so aren't disappointed if it doesn't. So long as we are kind they are usually very touched that we've prayed. Often they will experience something of the Holy Spirit even if they don't realise it or get healed.

Earlier this year a friend of ours was having a skiing lesson. As he travelled down the slope behind the instructor he "saw" a dark shadow over her hip. At the end of the lesson, after they'd been chatting for a while, he asked her, "Have you ever damaged your hip?" The lady replied that she'd been in an accident, injured her hip and that she'd never really recovered from it. Our friend offered to pray for her. He said a brief prayer, spoke to the hip and commanded that it be healed. Nothing particularly happened in that moment.

Later in the week he arranged another lesson with the same instructor. This time the moment she saw him her whole demeanour had changed. She was incredibly open. She started telling him about problems she was having with her children, she opened up about other struggles going on in her life and he was able to share a little about Jesus in response. The woman's hip hadn't been healed but somehow there had been a breakthrough. As the lesson was drawing to an end she turned to our friend and said, "Thank you so much for offering to pray for me. *No one has ever offered to pray for me.*"

EVERYDAY COURAGE

Even praying for people we know requires courage, and to keep going requires perseverance. If, like us, you feel your fears may get the better of you, we'd suggest praying for boldness. Supernatural boldness has nothing to do with our personalities; it is something God gives to those who ask him.

Although the day of Pentecost seems to have transformed the disciples from fearful to fearless, we still read that they continued to pray for courage. We've already pointed out that they asked God for signs and wonders, but this went hand in hand with asking for boldness: "Now, Lord, consider their threats and enable your servants to speak your word with great boldness. Stretch out your hand to heal and perform signs and wonders through the name of your holy servant Jesus" (Acts 4:29–30).

Our hope in moving forwards in this is not in our own grit or determination, it is in asking God to partner with us and transform us. He is always willing to give us, his children, what we need to step out.

GO ...

We want to finish this chapter with one final story.

A friend of ours, Debby Wright, leads the Vineyard movement in the UK with her husband John. She is amazing at stepping out and praying for people. One of the reasons we find her so encouraging is she makes it seem so normal and so doable!

About nine months before the time of writing Debby went to collect a parcel from a neighbour, Emma.[1] They had never met and so she introduced herself and they had a little chat. Debby then returned home and sat down to have her quiet time. As she sat down she felt what she described as a "flicker" or a "butterfly" and the words "acid reflux condition". She thought, *That must be for Emma*. After some deliberation—it's so easy not to pay attention to these things—she decided to go back round and ask. She rang the doorbell, and when her neighbour answered she said, "Hey, Emma, I've come back because I'm a Christian and sometimes Jesus speaks to me. I've just had a little impression and the words 'acid reflux condition'. Is this something you have?" Emma was amazed and said it was, she explained she was on pills for the condition and that there were quite a few foods she wasn't able to eat. When Debby offered to pray for healing, Emma invited her in.

Debby laid a hand on Emma's tummy. She invited the Holy Spirit but didn't take long and she spoke to the condition. She commanded the acid reflux to stop and for Emma's body to become receptive to the foods it was reacting to. It didn't take more than a couple of minutes. Afterwards, Debby told Emma to make sure she didn't come off any medication, but suggested that she try a few different foods and visit the doctor if she noticed any improvement. She said, "Thanks so much for letting me pray for you," and left.

Debby didn't see Emma for several months and then one day there was a knock at the door. It was Emma. She was smiling as she said, "You're not going to believe this," (to which Debby said, "I think I am"), "I have been eating everything I want to eat. I'm now off the medication, we've just come back from an all-inclusive holiday and we've eaten everything. We always used to go self-catering because I had to have special food but now I'm totally better. Whatever it is you did, one of those 'impressions' you talked about, if you ever get it again you've got to do it to other people." Debby said, "I didn't do anything, it was the power of Jesus." Since then they've met up a few times, Emma is not yet a Christian but she is on a journey.

Both of us are inspired by people like Debby. We feel inadequate and unsuccessful when it comes to power evangelism. We are, however, realising that we've made it harder than it needs to be. We have resolved to step out in praying for the people we know and grow into praying for those we don't. Debby and others demonstrate that if we make a mistake, or the person isn't healed, the kingdom can still be advanced. People are almost always touched when we offer to pray.

We are Jesus's ambassadors. He sends us out to advance his kingdom. We go with his authority and with the Holy Spirit. Let us grow into followers who proclaim the kingdom and who demonstrate the kingdom. Let's be the one who offers to pray.

11

GROWING IN FAITH

I do believe; help my unbelief!

Mark 9:24 (NASB)

It took a lot to catch Jesus off guard. He was, after all, God. Jesus was able to look at the Samaritan woman and tell her how many husbands she'd had. He sent the disciples off to find donkeys, spare rooms and fish that had swallowed coins, all of which he had supernatural knowledge of. He easily saw through the tricks of the Pharisees when they tried to trap him, and he had the ability to discern people's hearts; he saw the good in people he'd just met and the evil intentions of others.

IMPRESSING JESUS

Jesus understood the future. Long before he was arrested, he was clear that the Jews would crucify him, that Judas would betray him, that Peter would deny knowing him and that the disciples would all abandon him. He had wisdom far greater than Solomon. The morality of much of the West has since been founded on his teaching.

Finally, to top this all off, everything and everyone who has existed has been held together in him. We are held "in him" right now. It probably would have been a bit tricky to throw him a surprise birth-day party.

Yet Jesus could be shocked. It didn't happen often, In fact, the Gospels record only two times when Jesus was amazed.

The first instance is in Mark 6:5–6. Jesus had been travelling around Lake Galilee healing the sick, casting out demons and preaching. He then headed to his hometown, Nazareth, to con-tinue ministering. Perhaps Jesus had expected even more to happen in Nazareth, but the opposite occurred. Instead of his friends and neighbours believing in him, they were offended by him. Mark tells us, "He could not do any miracles there, except lay his hands on a few sick people and heal them. He was amazed at their lack of faith." It must have been a low point for Jesus and the disciples. The Baptist preacher Charles Spurgeon calls this "The Sad Wonder". Jesus didn't wonder at the size of the grandeur of the buildings in Jerusalem, he was never astounded by anyone's intelligence or impressed by the success of the Roman Empire. The lack of belief in Nazareth, how-ever, left him shaking his head in astonishment.

The second instance occurred when Jesus was walking through Capernaum. Some Jewish elders approached him, begging him to come and heal the servant of a Roman centurion. Jesus didn't take much persuading, and off they went. Before they could get to the house, however, the centurion sent his friends to Jesus with a mes-sage: "'Lord, don't trouble yourself, for I do not deserve to have you come under my roof. That is why I did not even consider myself worthy to come to you. But say the word, and my servant will be healed.' … When Jesus heard this, he was amazed at him …" This centurion sent Jesus a message that stunned him. The Greek word is *thaumazo*, which means, "to be extraordinarily impressed or disturbed by something."[1] Another way of translating "amazed" might be "wondered", "marvelled" or "was taken aback". Turning to the crowd who were following, Jesus explained his reaction, "I tell you, I have not found such great faith even in Israel" (Luke 7:6–7, 9).

As Spurgeon said, "That Jesus marvelled was in itself a marvel."[2] The Son of God, who knew about spouse-counts, money-eating-cod and people's innermost thoughts, could be stunned. In both instances it was faith, or the absence of it, that caused him to wonder.

HOW TO PLEASE GOD

Plenty of other instances make the power of faith clear. Jesus often encouraged people to trust him more. "You of little faith" is a phrase he used to admonish his followers on more than one occasion (Matt. 6:30; 8:26; 14:31; 16:8). Once, after failing to cast out a demon, the disciples asked why they couldn't do it. Jesus replied, "Because you have so little faith. Truly I tell you, if you have faith as small as a mustard seed, you can say to this mountain, 'Move from here to there,' and it will move. Nothing will be impossible for you" (Matt. 17:20).

In contrast, wherever Jesus found people with faith he praised them and power was also released. He said to the woman with the bleeding problem, "Daughter, your faith has healed you" (Mark 5:34). He was deeply impressed by the faith of another non-Jew, a Canaanite woman, "Woman, you have great faith! Your request is granted" (Matt. 15:28). Much of Jesus's attitude to faith is captured by Hebrews 11:6: "Without faith it is impossible to please God, because anyone who comes to him must believe that he exists and that he rewards those who earnestly seek him."

So, we are told that without faith it is impossible to please God and with faith, nothing will be impossible for us. Faith must be important!

SURPRISINGLY GOOD NEWS

It is easy to read these passages with a sinking feeling, and we can end up disqualifying ourselves because of our doubts. Both of us are quietly thankful that our "faith level" isn't displayed on a dashboard for all to see!

Jesus's teaching on faith, however, is actually wonderfully—and surprisingly—good news. It means the final responsibility for advancing God's kingdom doesn't rest with us. We aren't to put an expectation on ourselves to heal people, or set them free, or lead them to Jesus. This is beyond us. Instead, *we need to trust that God can do it through us.* When we understand this all the pressure is lifted from our shoulders. The burden now rests with God. Imagine we had to lift up a car to change the tyre. If we tried to do it in our own strength we'd end up in hospital. We need a jack because only the jack has the power to lift the car. Only God himself has the power to lift sickness and bring revelation—in this (irreverent) example he is the jack. The faith-filled Christian is one who trusts that the jack can take the weight. They lift the car but they know it's the jack (not their own biceps) doing the real work. To put it another way, the faith-filled Christian is one who can step out, trusting that as they do so God will do the heavy lifting.

Having said this, all of us will struggle with doubt sometimes. Jesus's twelve disciples certainly had their moments and this is part of the normal Christian life. Wrestling through doubt is part of the reality of the everyday supernatural. A life of faith isn't one free from all doubt, it's one where we keep expecting God to be faithful in the midst of our questions.

Both of us can connect with the man who brought his demonised son to Jesus, asking if he *could* do anything. "'If you can"?' said Jesus. 'Everything is possible for one who believes.' Immediately the boy's father exclaimed, 'I do believe; help me overcome my unbelief!'" (Mark 9:23–24). This is how many of us feel much of the time. We do believe and we do trust, but we long to trust God more. We have faith but we want our faith to increase. How does that happen?

WHAT IS FAITH?

Faith isn't something we can fake. The two of us have heard teaching that says we should only ever speak positively. That if we have the flu we shouldn't say we have the flu; we should say we have the *symptoms* of the flu (apparently admitting you take Lemsip is admitting you aren't living in Christ's power). The same teaching suggests that if we start proclaiming we have health, wealth and happiness before we have them, then we will receive them. This isn't biblical faith; it's just playing word games. If Lazarus had told himself he wasn't dead, he just had the *symptoms* of death, we aren't sure it would have made much difference.

The trouble with such teaching is that it elevates faith in the wrong way. When we spend all our time and energy focused on our own "faith level" we've totally missed it. We've put our faith in "faith". Our eyes should be on Jesus instead.

Faith is really about two things: trusting God's character, and stepping out because of this trust.

GOD'S CHARACTER

True faith is *a deep-rooted trust in God's character*. Knowing this explains why faith matters so much. It's not firstly about miracles or healing, it's about relationship. The key to intimacy in any relationship isn't sight or touch; it's trust. Two people can share a bed and yet not trust each other; their bodies may be close but their hearts are thousands of miles apart. Conversely, two people can be on opposite sides of the world but, if they trust each other, they can still have intimacy. Faith is trusting God. It's having our hearts invested in him. This sort of faith is not something that can be hyped up or manipulated into existence, but it can grow. Put another way, "Faith is loyalty to Jesus."[3] Growing in faith then, is ultimately about learning to know, lean into and depend upon his character.

STEPPING OUT

In his letter, James writes, "Faith without deeds is dead" (James 2:26). By this he means that faith is a verb; it's a "doing word". In Mark 2 Jesus was sitting in someone's house when bits of the roof started to fall in. As the dust fell, sky began to appear overhead and a short time later so did the faces of five men peering down at them. Eventually the friends of a paralytic man lowered him through the hole they'd made and he landed at Jesus's feet. Verse 5 reads, "When Jesus saw their faith ..." What was the giveaway that these men had faith? Was the word stamped on their foreheads? No, it was the hole in the roof. Faith is an action and these men would have done anything to get their friend to the man they believed could heal him.

Sometimes we have to act even when we can't sense God's presence, and the circumstances look bleak. Real faith is stepping out of the boat, trusting Jesus will hold you up just like he did Peter during the storm.

Charles Blondin (real name Jean-Francois Gravelet) was a famous tightrope walker who lived in the 1800s. One of his most impressive stunts was to cross Niagara Falls on a thin length of wire. As part of his act he would ask the crowd, "Do you believe I can do this?" "Yes," they would all shout, "you can do it!" Then Blondin would walk back and forth across the tightrope. The crowd would go wild. He would then say, "Now I'm going to do it with a wheelbarrow. Do you believe I can do it?" The crowd would all clap and cheer, roaring him on. He would walk the 1,100 feet back and forth. Then for the big finale, Blondin would say, "Now I'm going to put someone in the wheelbarrow and take them over. Do you believe I can do it?" The crowd would scream and yell, "Yes, yes, we believe!" Then Blondin would ask for a volunteer. At this point there was always dead silence. The crowd claimed they trusted Blondin, but when it came to that faith being tested by action, it failed. True faith means climbing out of the boat, or volunteering to get into the wheelbarrow.

THE FAITHFUL ONE

If faith begins with trusting God's character, the best way to grow faith is to get to know him better. Imperfect faith in God always comes from imperfect knowledge of God.

If someone were to promise us £100,000 and we didn't trust that person's character, we would soon forget about the promise. If we knew the person well, if we were convinced they were reliable, then we would get very excited! God has promised us far more than £100,000. Often we aren't excited about his promises because we don't appreciate the fact that God is always true to his word. He is totally kind, faithful and loving.

Mike

In the summer of 2004 Soul Survivor organised ten days of mission in London call Soul in the City (which I mentioned in chapter 8). We had 11,500 young people taking part and we worked alongside 770 partner churches in the city. In the run up to the mission it became increasingly obvious that we were facing a huge financial shortfall running into hundreds of thousands of pounds. One of my friends approached a very wealthy businessman on our behalf, asking if he would help with the deficit. He declined, saying that we should never have undertaken the mission, God had not told us to do it and therefore we would go bankrupt.

When I heard this I was devastated. I convinced myself that we had somehow been disobedient to God, that we had not prayed enough, that I was not holy enough and bankruptcy would be God's punishment. I used to write a regular article in a Christian magazine and the deadline for the September issue was just before Soul in the City was due to begin at the end of August. I wrote the article with a heavy heart. I began, "By the time you read this article Soul Survivor will probably be bankrupt," and listed all the possible reasons why I believed this might happen.

I then spoke to my friend Matt Redman about the words of the businessman and my fears. Matt responded by saying something like this: "Mike, we all prayed about this and sincerely believed the Lord was telling us to do this mission. Even if we were wrong, all we are trying to do is reach people in London with the gospel. Surely that isn't such a terrible thing. And anyway, this idea that God wants to punish us by causing us to go bankrupt, does that really sound like the voice of our Father?"

Matt's words cut me to the heart. For a short time, I had lost sight of my Father's goodness, mercy and compassion. As I remembered who he is, the fog began to lift.

The mission proved to be a wonderful time and by the final day every penny we needed had come in, sometimes in miraculous ways. Another businessman saw what we were doing and promptly wrote a cheque for £100,000. We rejoiced in God's faithfulness. For a while people even started affirming what a man of "faith and power" I must be for holding my nerve against the odds. And then in September the magazine came out.

———————

We get to know God by reading his Word; it's hard to spend much time in the Bible without discovering more about his heart. Mark describes an occasion when a leper approached Jesus (Mark 1:40–45). The word *leprosy* would have had a broader meaning then than it does now, but at its worst it is a skin condition that can cause people to be horribly disfigured. At the time of Jesus it was incurable. Moreover, because of the Jewish ceremonial law, those who had leprosy were shunned. They were regarded as "unclean"; people would have crossed the street to avoid going near them. When this man drew near to Jesus he fell on his knees and began to beg him, "If you are willing, you can make me clean" (v. 40). He had no doubts about whether Jesus was *able* to help him. His question was whether Jesus was *willing* to help him. Many of us are in the same position, we trust that God is *powerful enough*, but we doubt whether he is *willing enough* to help.

Jesus's reaction says everything: "Jesus was *indignant*. He reached out his hand and touched the man. 'I am willing,' he said. 'Be clean!'" (vv. 40–41). The word translated "indignant" in Greek sounds crazy, *splagchnizomai* (try ordering that at the next Pizza Hut you visit). It means a deep feeling or a yearning that comes from the guts. Another translation might be that Jesus was "moved with compassion." Jesus was clearly deeply stirred by the man's fear that he wouldn't heal him. *Am I willing?* Jesus may have thought, "You are a social outcast, you have a horrific skin condition, you are begging me for help and you want to know if I'm willing? We clearly haven't met ..."

John Wimber used to tell the story of how he began to see God heal people. After six months of praying for people his church hadn't seen anyone get healed. They would take hours and hours to pray for one person and see not even the slightest bit of improvement. Sometimes they would actually catch the diseases of the sick people they were praying for! Then suddenly the breakthrough came. John was more surprised than anyone when a woman he prayed for immediately recovered.

This was the beginning of a remarkable move of God that spread to many parts of the world. The day John saw his first miracle of healing God also gave him a vision. It was a picture of the sky transformed into a great honeycomb. Honey was dripping from the comb and landing all over the ground. People had different reactions to the honey. Some people were disgusted by it, they were scraping it off themselves and trying to get clean. They weren't happy about the mess it was making. Others were cupping their hands and trying to catch as much of it as they could. They were eating it and sharing it with those around them. God said to John, "That's a picture of my mercy, John. You don't need to ever beg me for healing again. The problem is not at my end."

God was drawing John's attention to his overwhelming willingness to act on our behalf. He is far more willing to shower us with blessing than we are to ask him for it. The leper who asked Jesus for healing clearly didn't know his character; he didn't understand Jesus's compassion. Note the next thing Jesus did after he's healed the man: "Jesus sent him away at once with a strong warning: 'See that you don't tell this to anyone'" (vv. 43–44).

It's fascinating that on this and many other occasions Jesus told the people he's healed to keep their mouths shut. If we healed someone of leprosy we'd probably get them to make a YouTube video about it and hope it went viral. But Jesus wasn't interested in the publicity. His motivation for making people whole wasn't to impress others, it was simply compassion for the person standing in front of him. He did it just for them.

Let's take a step back for a moment and look again at the God of the Bible. He is a God who gives to an unfathomable extent. Imagine for a moment wanting a child of your own and reading about Andy's son Josiah. You think he sounds pretty great and so you arrive at Andy and Beth's home and ask whether they would give him to you. Do you think they would? Of course not! Yet we worship a God who has freely given us his beloved son Jesus. Not only to live with us but to die for us. What does this mean? Paul puts it like this in Romans 8:32: "He who did not spare his own Son, but gave him up for us all—how will he not also, along with him, graciously give us all things?"

Increasing our faith is simply a case of realising the truth about who God is. Our faith expands as we come to recognise God as the Faithful One. When we come to ask him to heal, to save, to help, do we really think God isn't willing? If we do, then we don't understand his character. It is one of goodness, mercy and compassion. The promises of Scripture matter because of the character of the one who makes them. "Let us hold unswervingly to the hope we profess, for *he who promised is faithful*" (Heb. 10:23).

EXERCISING YOUR FAITH MUSCLE

The two of us like to go to the gym together and we like to compete. Over the years we've been competing on the bench press (Andy feels that it's important you know that at the time of writing he is winning).

When attempting to build muscle we have found two things to be true. First, muscles have to be exercised to breaking point, they need to be pushed beyond what is comfortable. Only when this happens does the muscle tear and when it tears it regrows bigger and stronger. Faith is like a muscle. The only way faith is grown is as we exercise it. We have to act, often to a point where it doesn't feel comfortable.

Secondly, a muscle increases in strength as it is consistently exercised over time. It isn't possible to go from bench-pressing 90 kg to 190 kg in one week (we know; we've tried it). The way to increase the amount we can lift is to work towards it. In the same way faith doesn't dramatically skyrocket in just a few days. The secret is to regularly step out over a long period of time. We should be encouraged that wherever we start from we can develop strong faith; we just have to patiently and persistently exercise it.

ACT ON WHAT YOU HAVE

Often we make the mistake of waiting to "receive" more faith before we step out in obedience. If we do this, we miss the fact that faith is received by our acting on what we already have. Smith Wigglesworth said, "If you act with what you have, your faith will be increased. You can never increase your faith *but* by acting."[4]

Let's put it another way. Taking a step of faith often feels like standing on the edge of a diving board. The pool is twenty feet beneath us and it's empty. We may feel like God is saying, "Jump!" (That could mean any number of things in the everyday supernatural: praying for that person, sharing the gospel with that person, giving your colleague a prophetic word you think you've had for him or her.) Our response is usually, "Okay, God, you fill the pool with water and then I'll jump." God says, "No, you jump and then I'll fill the pool with water." Acting in faith is obeying what we think God is saying without knowing exactly how it will end.

Acts of faith always involve an element of risk. Someone once said "faith" is spelt R-I-S-K. We all want to be 100 per cent sure that we've heard God correctly before we take a step of faith, but most of the time it doesn't work like that. The ethics teacher John Kavanaugh once visited Mother Teresa in Calcutta. He asked her to pray that God might give him clarity. Mother Teresa said firmly, "No. I will not do that." He was surprised and asked why. She explained, "I have never had clarity; what I have always had is trust. So I will pray that you trust God."[5]

If we get caught up in the hunt for clarity our faith will never grow. We aren't saying that we should rush into taking huge risks on a whim; we only step out when we think God has spoken. Yet knowing God often speaks in whispers means we should make trust and action our goal. We'll get it wrong at times, but more often than not, we'll find there is water in the pool after all!

JUMPING OFF THE DIVING BOARD

Andy

A few years ago I was invited to share the gospel at a carol service at Oxford University. The Christian Union runs the service each year and it is held in the Sheldonian Theatre, a stunning Grade I listed building in the heart of the city. It was a great privilege to be asked, but a little daunting—I am more used to speaking in the industrial warehouse where our church meets.

The night before the service I was sitting in bed reading my Bible and felt prompted to turn to Psalm 71. I didn't know the psalm well and so was hugely comforted to read,

> Since my youth, God, you have taught me,
>   and to this day I declare your marvellous
>   deeds.
> Even when I am old and grey,
>   do not forsake me, my God,
> till I declare your power to the next generation,
>   your mighty acts to all who are to come.
>   (vv. 17–18)

That was my prayer to God and it felt like he was saying, "I'm here, Andy. I've got you."

The next morning, I began to prepare my talk. I planned to spend the whole day working on it before driving over to Oxford to speak that night. I don't know if you've ever had a total mind-blank at an important moment but that's what happened as I sat down to write. I couldn't think of a single thing to say! I started to panic and that made things worse. As the day wore on and the time to leave drew closer I was staring at a blank screen, thinking, *You moron, you are about to speak to hundreds of Oxford University students and you have nothing to say to them.*

Throughout the day I kept reading Psalm 71 aloud in an attempt to cheer myself up. It didn't really work. The time came when I had to leave and I just had a few scribbled thoughts on a piece of paper. Mike and Beth were so worried about me they decided to come along for support. We drove to Oxford in total silence so that I could prepare. When we arrived I left Mike and Beth to park the car and I said I needed to be alone. I walked into the Sheldonian Theatre and as I was an hour early, I went and hid in the toilet!

I sat locked in the cubicle for a whole hour trying to gather my thoughts. I read Psalm 71 aloud again and again, saying, "Lord, please help." I also tried to write the talk but my brain seemed to have gone into hibernation and I couldn't come up with anything. My dad went to Oxford University, so I texted him telling him where I was and saying I was a bit nervous and would appreciate some prayer. He texted back, "I'm praying for you, and also I have a picture of the Holy Spirit resting on you and all the fear leaving." It was a nice text to receive but the Holy Spirit didn't seem like he was in Oxford, let alone in my cubicle.

The service started and I had no choice but to get up and speak. I was terrified until the moment I opened my mouth, but when I started to speak, suddenly God's peace arrived. I shared as honestly as I could about who Jesus is and what knowing him means. I'm under no illusions that the talk was amazing—but considering the few thoughts I had scribbled on my piece of paper, it seemed like a total miracle. Mike and Beth came up to me afterwards, astonished and relieved that it had come together. Driving back that night I was ashamed at how much I had doubted God's ability to help me but grateful that he'd been faithful anyway.

The following morning, I texted dad again. I told him it had gone well and also said, "You should check out Psalm 71, it's a good one." My dad, who is ordained, texted straight back, "I know, it's a great one; it was the reading in our chapel service last night. We read it aloud and prayed for you by name."

It may seem a small thing to you as you read this, but to me it meant the world. I was sitting in a toilet cubicle in Oxford reading Psalm 71 aloud. My dad was sitting in a chapel in another part of the country reading aloud the very same psalm and praying for me. It felt like God saying, "DO YOU GET IT, ANDY?"

That was one "diving board" moment for me. In that instance I *had* to jump off because I'd committed to speaking months earlier. We'll all have our own versions of stepping out, whether it's sharing a prophetic word or reaching out to a colleague at work or praying for a relative at home. For all of us, it will feel like risk. The Asaro tribe of Indonesia and Papua New Guinea has a saying, "Knowledge is only a rumour until it lives in a muscle."[7] It means what we understand about "faith" is only a theory until it becomes part of our lived experience. There's no substitute for stepping out and finding in our moment of vulnerability, that God is able to carry us. It's the best, and only, place for faith to be exercised and strengthened.

FROM FAITH TO FEAR TO FAITH

Only one person in the Bible is known as the "father" of those in the faith: Abraham (Rom. 4:16), and he is listed as one of the great heroes of the faith in Hebrews 11. God promised him countless descendants even though he and his wife Sarah were barren and far too old to have children. Romans 4:3 says, "Abraham believed God, and it was credited to him as righteousness." Given that he's such a legend in the faith we might have expected him to have a pretty smooth trajectory from faith to ever-increasing faith. He didn't.

We find his full story in Genesis, beginning at chapter 12. Though he believed God when God spoke to him, Abraham had many moments when he wavered and doubted. Often when God makes a promise there is a delay before that promise is fulfilled. It is in this in-between period that God tests our faith and refines our hearts. For Abraham, when the fulfillment of the promise of a son was delayed, he decided to help God out. He slept with his wife's servant Hagar and as a result she gave birth to Ishmael. Big mistake.

On another occasion (Gen. 20), the great man of faith became so afraid of King Abimelek that he told him that Sarah was his sister and not his wife. The king came very close to sleeping with her. When we read the summary of Abraham's life in Hebrews 11 we see him as a great man of faith. When we read the full story in Genesis, however, we are told clearly that he wavered between fear and faith quite regularly.

Yet Abraham kept coming back to God despite his fears and God kept hold of him in spite of his failures. Abraham's faith was refined on the journey so that by the end he had learned to trust even when he didn't understand all of God's instructions or actions. We see the culmination of this in Genesis 22 when God told Abraham to take Isaac, the son of promise, up a mountain and kill him.

God was testing Abraham's ability to trust and Abraham magnificently passed this final test. Abraham's faith had been strengthened through the wobbles. As we seek to grow in faith we can draw comfort from Abraham—he ended up the father of faith, but he had his fair share of doubts along the way. What matters is that when we hit a bump, make a mistake or give in to doubt, we quickly come back to God. It is his kindness, not our faith, that is our ultimate hope.

THE PERFECTER OF FAITH

It's important that we finish by underlining something we've said throughout this book. The way to live an everyday supernatural life is to be close to Jesus. This is the only way faith grows. We can't increase faith through our own efforts any more than we can decide to grow a new set of teeth. Yet we can make space for it in our lives by spending time in the Bible and allowing God to reveal his character to us.

We can also step out and obey the things that we believe God is saying, as the more we obey, the more we get to know Jesus's character and our trust in him increases. It's a cycle. Faith is based on total trust in Jesus and so the nearer we are to him, the greater it grows. Like Abraham we may have triumphs of faith-filled moments and valleys of seemingly bottomless doubts, but being confident of who God is, "let us run with perseverance the race marked out for us, fixing our eyes on Jesus, the pioneer and perfecter of faith" (Heb. 12:1–2).

12

SUSTAINING THE SUPERNATURAL

Let perseverance finish its work so that you may be
mature and complete, not lacking anything.

James 1:4

It can be easy to read a book like this, get excited, and have a go for a few weeks. Then when the enthusiasm dies down, and if we don't see all that we hoped, we can give up. For the everyday supernatural to truly become a new normal there is one more characteristic we need to consider: perseverance.

"Success" in the everyday supernatural isn't about getting everything right; it's about keeping going. The biblical word for this is "perseverance" and it is an essential character trait for a Christian.

James writes, "Consider it pure joy, my brothers and sisters, whenever you face trials of many kinds, because you know that the testing of your faith produces perseverance. Let perseverance finish its work so that you may be mature and complete, not lacking anything" (James 1:2–4). This seems incredibly counter-intuitive.

Rejoice when it's hard? Be cheerful when there is opposition, trials and testing? What on earth is James talking about?

He is on the hunt for something that brings about maturity. He says persevering shapes us into mature Christians, and perseverance can *only* be developed when we are tested. In living out the everyday supernatural, our faith will be tested *every day*, so just think of all the perseverance we are going to develop!

THE CROSS-LIFE

Dietrich Bonhoeffer famously said, "When Christ calls a man he bids him come and die."[1] He was referring to Jesus's statement "Whoever wants to be my disciple must deny themselves and take up their cross daily and follow me" (Luke 9:23). Jesus didn't float around on a cloud throwing healing powder on people. He was involved in the mess and grime of their lives. Isaiah describes him as "a man of suffering, and familiar with pain" (Isa. 53:3).

When the Holy Spirit filled Jesus, it wasn't to give him an easy life on earth; on the contrary, the Holy Spirit empowered Jesus to face suffering for the sake of others. When the Spirit anointed Jesus at his baptism the very next thing that happened was that the Spirit led him into the desert. Jesus began a time of testing and trial at the hands of Satan.

When Jesus returned and stood up in the synagogue in Nazareth he proclaimed, "The Spirit of the Lord is on me" (Luke 4:18). In other words, "Watch out world—you are about to see what a Spirit-filled-everyday-supernatural-life looks like!" He continued, "Because he has anointed me to proclaim good news to the poor. He has sent me to proclaim freedom for the prisoners and recovery of sight for the blind, to set the oppressed free ..." (v. 18). The Spirit-filled life, as modelled by Jesus, is one where we selflessly give ourselves to the poor, the prisoner, the blind, the oppressed and anyone else who needs help. As the Spirit draws us into the work of advancing Jesus's kingdom so we'll find ourselves drawn towards dying to self and living for others. This, after all, is what praying for the sick, sharing prophetic words, and telling people the gospel is all about.

Thomas Smail wrote, "The Spirit *comes from* the Cross and the Spirit *leads us* to the Cross."[2] This isn't because the goal of the everyday supernatural is suffering for its own sake. The goal is loving people, and the love of Jesus is sacrificial. When you love, you sacrifice. When you love, you persevere. The mother of a newborn baby is often sleep deprived, exhausted and for months lives life at full stretch. She will probably have to get up many times each night to feed and change her baby. It is a sacrifice. Yet her love for her baby makes the sacrifice worthwhile.

There is an intimacy with God that comes not only when we gaze at him in worship but also when we walk with him in sacrificial ministry. When he gives us his love for people we will sacrifice our time, our comfort and our energy in order to see them blessed.

THE GIFT OF PLODDING

Another of our spiritual heroes is a man called William Carey. He became convinced that it was the job of Christians to share the gospel with people around the world—at that time not everyone thought this—and went to India as a missionary in 1793.

William's life was not exactly a bed of roses—three of his seven children died in childhood, his wife developed a severe mental illness, and William himself suffered a skin condition that meant he couldn't be out in direct sunlight. He didn't see anyone converted for the first *seven years* of his ministry in India, and lost six years' worth of work in one night when the manuscripts he had been labouring on were destroyed in a fire. However, by the end of his life he had seen thousands come to know God and had opened up a way for missionaries to go throughout India. Over the years he translated the Bible into Bengali, Oriya, Assamese, Arabic, Hindi and Sanskrit.

It's hard to articulate the impact of his life, and he is now celebrated as the "father of modern missions". His famous motto was, "Expect great things from God, attempt great things for God." That is what he did, day after day, and setback after setback. Towards the end of his life, William was asked what his greatest gift was. He replied, "If people would ask, 'What was Mr Carey's greatest gift?' I would have them told, 'Mr Carey's greatest gift was that he knew how to plod.'"

Sustaining the everyday supernatural is about learning how to plod. It's about being open to what the Spirit might be saying to us, surrendered to his will and ready to step out. The great need of the church isn't for a few one-off risk-takers, it's for risk-taking plodders.

When John Wimber used to teach about healing, some listeners would attempt to pray for people a few times, then they would come back to Wimber and say, "It doesn't work. No one I prayed for was healed." Wimber's response was always, "Go and pray for a thousand people and then we'll talk." He knew that if they prayed for a thousand people they wouldn't need to chat as they would have seen people healed. If we really want this to become the new normal we need to choose to live in this place every day. If we make the decision to plod today, in fifty years' time we'll be rejoicing that we did!

HOW TO KEEP GOING

Plodding is harder some days than others. We'll all have times when we struggle and feel like quitting, so how do we keep on keeping on? Here are a few things that have helped us persevere.

DO IT TOGETHER

The writer to the Hebrews encouraged his readers, "Let us consider how we may spur one another on towards love and good deeds, not giving up meeting together, as some are in the habit of doing, but encouraging one another" (Heb. 10:24–25).

The greatest character in the Old Testament (after God), is not Abraham, or Moses, or David, it's Israel: a people, not a person. The greatest character in the New Testament after Jesus is the church. God puts us into the family of the church because he knows we need one another. As we come to the end of this book it is important to ask, "How am I going to live out the everyday supernatural life?" and "With whom am I going to live it out?" We are to spur one another on.

We hope this doesn't sound too cheesy but over the years both of us have found a deep strength in our friendship. Individually, as we've sought to obey God, we have had moments where we've felt close to despair. On occasions we've wanted to give up. We've had times of self-doubt or when the enemy has attacked us and we haven't realised what has been going on. There have been instances where we have both felt like failures. In these moments we have been able to support one another. Instead of giving up we've drawn immense comfort from the fact we are a team and we are not alone. When David was on the run from Saul he had one of his darkest moments and it was his friend Jonathan who kept him going. It was Jonathan who "helped him find strength in God" (1 Sam. 23:16).

In the TV series *The West Wing*, there's a scene where Toby, the White House communications director, gives a speech to the entire communications staff. He says, "We're a team. From the president … on through, we're a team. We win together, we lose together. We celebrate and we mourn together. And defeats are softened and victories sweeter because we did them together … You're my guys and I'm yours … and there's nothing I wouldn't do for you."[3] It's a great picture of how we go far in the everyday supernatural life. If we want to go fast it's best to go alone, but if we want to go far we need to go together. Ask God, "Who can I be a friend to, who can I encourage to grow in these things? Who can I be a team with?"

STAY CLOSE

If we're not careful even the most passionate among us can lose our zeal. For a fire to keep burning it needs to constantly be fed.

Our priority needs to be sticking close to Jesus. Before being everyday supernatural is about miracles and healings, it's about intimacy and relationship. One way to stay close to the Lord is quality time. For most of us this won't look like hours in prayer but it should look like regularly being together. The psalmist writes,

Blessed is the one …

whose delight is in the law of the LORD,

    and who meditates on his law day and night.

That person is like a tree planted by streams of water,

    which yields its fruit in season

and whose leaf does not wither. (Ps. 1:1–3)

The image of the slow-growing, fruit-bearing tree is helpful; we want long and sustained growth. The way to do this is to draw near to God—the psalmist suggests day and night. It's that steady trickle from the stream that enables us to thrive. Reading God's Word helps. It can expand our horizons. It gives us direction for the way ahead, it reminds us of God's promises and it shows us again what's possible. Worshipping God ushers in his presence and it refreshes our souls. It keeps us looking to him, his mercy and his strength, rather than our own clay pots and shortcomings. Praying, or "keeping company with God," deepens our friendship with him and establishes his kingdom. It helps maintain the discipline of listening that is essential for everything else.

The more we develop and grow, the further we travel along the everyday supernatural, the more there is to see and know of Jesus. He rarely does the same thing twice. As we become more familiar with him we are more amazed by him. Sticking close to him is the only way for us to be satisfied and yet the more of him we know, the thirstier we will become for his presence. To sustain the everyday supernatural it's important to develop a daily pattern of drawing near to Jesus. Of course, we'll manage this better at some times than at others and that is normal, but let this be our ambition—one that we ask God to help us grow into.

PLANT SEEDS

After some time we can become discouraged in the everyday supernatural if we feel like we are not seeing the "results" we hoped for.
One of the things that we need to keep coming back to is that "success" is obedience to God. A good day is one where we've followed
the lead of the Spirit as best we can. Often we won't see immediate
results. In the parable of the sower, many of the seeds don't end up
in the good soil but the farmer throws them out anyway. The more
seeds we plant the more of a harvest we'll reap. It's impossible to
know what might happen as a result of our stepping out; often much
more happens than can be seen on the surface.

Mike

In 1997 I spoke at a youth camp situated by a beautiful lake in central Finland. One afternoon a sixteen-year-old called Timo asked to
talk to me. We sat on a bench overlooking the lake and Timo told me
his story. It was tragic. His father was an alcoholic and used to come
home drunk and beat Timo and his mother. The boy felt powerless
to defend either himself or his mum. Then, when Timo was nine, his
father left home and never returned. Timo told me that he had no
idea where his dad was or whether he was even alive. He told me that
he felt both angry and depressed and struggled to believe in God's
Father-love for him.

I prayed with Timo and we agreed we would meet again the next
day. The following afternoon I was wearing my favourite sweater. I
loved that sweater. It looked great and was comfortable and warm.

As we sat on the bench overlooking the lake I noticed Timo shivering in his T-shirt. I sensed the Lord telling me to lend Timo my sweater. I resisted. The Lord insisted. Reluctantly I gave him the sweater. It was five sizes too big for the boy but he told me how much he liked it. To my dismay the Lord then told me to give Timo my sweater as a gift. I objected. The Lord insisted. Timo seemed delighted. I left for the airport minus my favourite jumper and not in the best of moods.

Sixteen years later I was back in Finland, speaking at a pastors' conference. Before my final talk, my translator told me he wanted to say something to the congregation. He stood up and said:

> My name is Timo and I am thirty-two years old. Sixteen years ago I went to a camp by a lake. Mike was the speaker but he doesn't remember me! I told him the story of my alcoholic father and how as a result I struggled to believe in and receive God's love for me. Mike listened to me over two afternoons. On the second afternoon I was cold and Mike gave me his sweater. Then he went back to England. What Mike doesn't know is that God used that sweater to change my life. My father had never given me any gifts and I was amazed when this stranger gave me such a great sweater. I began to think that maybe God was behind this gift and that maybe I could have hope that my life might change.

He then reached into a bag and took out my jumper. "I kept this for sixteen years," he said, "but today I give it back as it's done its job." I was stunned. I had no idea why God told me to give my sweater away and for sixteen years it had been a puzzle to me. Then God, in his grace, showed me what he was doing behind my back! The lesson? Keep being obedient. Keep on sowing seeds. Walk faithfully even when you don't see the results immediately. You never know what God might be up to.

STEP OUT TODAY

The final thing that can encourage us as we plod into the wonderful, everyday supernatural, is that we can take one day at a time. Every morning we wake up and we find the mercies of God are new. It can be comforting to change our mindset from thinking we need to take risks of obedience forever, to just trying to do it for the rest of the day. Then we do the same again tomorrow, and the next day. Sooner or later we'll discover that how we spend our days is, of course, how we are spending our lives. We couldn't think of a better way to spend life than ushering in the glory of God, reflecting to the world that not only is God alive but he loves each of us and wants to forgive, heal, strengthen and free people. The great call is to follow him, spending ourselves for his glory—and by that we mean, of course, for his goodness, his mercy and his compassion. To quote Mother Teresa, "Yesterday has gone. Tomorrow has not yet come. We only have today. Let us begin."[4]

EPILOGUE

Andy

When I was seventeen years old I was standing in the dinner queue in the "Loaves and Fishes" tent at a camp called Harvest. It was a Christian camp that I'd been dragged to by my friend Paddy who was more "into God" than I was. I called myself a Christian, and recently I'd been trying to live like one, but I was pretty new to it all. I definitely wasn't keen enough to want to go to camps.

While we were waiting to order our burgers someone joined us at the back of the line. I recognised him as one of the speakers. He started chatting to Paddy about football but I didn't say anything to him, bought my food and wandered off. As I left he caught me and said, "Excuse me, this might sound a little strange but I think God might have told me I should pray for you. Would that be okay?" I was a bit taken aback—this had never happened to me before. I muttered something along the lines of, "Yeah, that'd be okay I suppose." He asked if I'd be at the evening meeting and said he'd find me and pray for me there.

That night I watched this person preach. He invited people to receive prayer and lots of people went forward while I stayed where I was, observing what was going on. After a while the man walked over to where I was sitting. He knelt down and asked to pray. He prayed for my eyes, that I would start to see what God was doing, and for my ears, that I would begin to hear God's voice. He prayed for my mouth, that I would begin to speak out God's heart, and he prayed for me to grow in wisdom and in leadership. At the end he looked at me kindly and said, "I think God may have told me to support you in any way I can. If you ever want to get in touch, please do. If there's any way I can serve you I will."

That man was Mike, and this is how we met.

When I look back, it scares me how easy it would have been to miss this. I know now that Mike was at Harvest at the end of a long and exhausting stretch of ministry. He would also say he was there in the middle of a particularly difficult season in life. It would have been so easy for him to ignore God's whisper. I also know that this everyday supernatural encounter radically altered the trajectory of my life. I ended up spending a year at Soul Survivor, going to study theology, starting full-time ministry, getting ordained, and becoming joint senior pastor of the church Mike and I now lead. Much more significantly, I have been blessed with the most amazing friendship, I have met my incredible wife, and God has healed me in ways I can't begin to describe.

I'm so grateful to God that he intervenes in our lives. I'm grateful to Mike that he stepped out in obedience and took a risk. I'm personally more resolved than ever not to miss out on the joy and blessing we can bestow on others when we follow the Spirit's lead. Finally, when I reflect on all that God has done, I can't help but think of all the times I've had little thoughts like that and dismissed them. How many times I thought, *It's just me.*

No more. Now, God, show us your glory …

SPIRIT-LED SMALL GROUP GUIDE

WHAT IS A 'SPIRIT-LED' SMALL GROUP?

Andy:

It was a mild February evening; I drove to church feeling nervous. It was the first meeting of our new connect group and we were reading *Everyday Supernatural* together. I was nervous, not about how people would respond to the book (I already knew there would be complaints about Mike's jokes), but because I couldn't control the most important part of the evening. We were going to be talking about the presence of God. I had told everyone we wouldn't just be talking about it; we'd actually be making space for God to show up. The only problem with telling everyone that you are going to do that, is that you then have to do it…

People trickled in and introduced themselves to one another over tea and biscuits. We met in 'The Den,' a backroom of our church that should probably be called 'The Pit.' It has a mismatched collection of furniture, a large pile of children's toys shoved untidily into a corner and is always either boiling hot or freezing cold. An enormous six-foot teddy bear sits on a sofa at one end. Rooms with less atmosphere would be hard to find.

To begin, we each shared, a bit awkwardly, about why we'd committed to the group and some of our own story. We worshipped God for a while. Then I took a deep breath and invited the Holy Spirit. We stood there for quite some time in silence while not much happened. I quietly wondered whether this was going to be a disappointing evening. Then I noticed a lady standing opposite, she had her eyes closed and looked peaceful. I wandered over and prayed for her, asking God to meet with her. After a little while the Spirit began to rest on her gently. It was not dramatic, but it was real. I felt encouraged and excited; God was here! By the time I turned around several other people had begun to experience the Spirit's presence. Some of it was lovely and gentle, some of it less gentle, but that didn't matter, what mattered was that God had shown up!

We wandered around the room praying for each other and trying to 'join in' with what the Spirit seemed to be doing. At the time I had no idea what the Spirit was doing. Some people wept, others laughed, others just stood still with a settled calm on them, and others – like me – didn't experience anything. This went on for about thirty minutes, then, when people seemed to have received enough prayer we sat on our mismatched furniture, opened our Bibles and had a discussion about the presence of God. The six-foot teddy in the corner listened in. Afterwards I drove home not just relieved but elated. What had thrilled me was the combination of how *ordinary* it all seemed and yet how *divine* it was. I felt like we were on to something new - 'Spirit-led small groups'. Of course this was actually something very old! Since Pentecost, normal, broken believers have gathered in ordinary, pokey rooms and invited the Holy Living God to meet with them. He loves to meet with us. Wouldn't you love to meet with him?

RISK-TAKING

We (Mike and Andy) share a mutual love for the programme *The West Wing*. In one particular episode President Bartlett's Chief of Staff, Leo, is critically ill. During a discussion at the hospital bedside the two reminisce about the way in which Bartlett had invited Leo to take the job. Smiling they remember Bartlett's question to Leo; it wasn't *'Would you like this job?'* it was, *"Are you ready to jump off a cliff?"*

Our question to you is not, 'Would you like to lead a small group?' It is, "Are *you* ready to jump off a cliff?"

Are you ready to attempt to lead a small group, youth group or a gathering with a few friends that looks very different from what we typically do in our churches? It will look different because however much you plan and prepare for it, you are going to be relying on God turning up and doing what only God can do. There will be nothing you can do to make that happen, you can only make space and trust that God will do the rest.

Let us say at the outset: it will feel like a big risk but it will be worth it.

PRACTICING

We hope this is a somewhat 'dangerous' small group guide because our expectation is that you, and everyone else in the group, will be taken out of your comfort zone. At times you may be fearful and there is a high chance of you looking foolish.

Our ambition is not that people would read books about the spiritual gifts, but that people would *exercise* the spiritual gifts. We've noticed that people tend to get enthusiastic about these things in large meetings and at conferences, but struggle to translate that enthusiasm into lived practice in everyday life. As such, it's our hope that any small group that decides to read *Everyday Supernatural* aims not to simply discuss the contents but also to make space to practice the contents of each chapter. This booklet is a guide to what that might look like.

You may want to put the image of a book-reading club out of your mind. Discussion is going to be important – it is essential that we understand the Biblical foundations for what we are doing - but *practice* and *having a go* are going to be equally important. If you went to a class on first aid, cooking or playing the guitar, you would expect to actually attempt CPR, bake a Victoria sponge or play some music. A huge amount of learning happens in the doing. To quote an old Chinese proverb, 'I hear I forget, I see I remember, I do I understand.' The aim of this group is not going to be getting through a list of pre-set questions; it is about following what the Spirit says in the moment and practicing obedience. If, at the end of each session, people aren't metaphorically covered in bandages, baking powder and broken guitar strings then it may not have been a memorable lesson! People aren't signing up for book club but for band practice – we're going to be *doing it*.

HOW CAN I LEAD A GROUP LIKE THIS?

WHO CAN LEAD IT?

You can.

People's main objection to leading a group where space is made for the Holy Spirit is 'I don't really know what I'm doing.' If you were going to a cooking class, you'd expect the person leading to know how to bake!

We want to assure you that in that very 'weakness' lies your great strength as a small group leader, youth leader, or person-who-is-really-keen-and-forces-their-mates-to-chat-about-the-book-weekly.

If you don't feel like you know what you're doing, do it anyway and tell people that's how you feel. The best approach is to say to whatever group you gather, 'I don't know what I'm doing but I want to grow in these things; can we learn together?' Lead from a place of vulnerability and honesty. It will give others permission to admit that they also don't know what they are doing and you can then enjoy figuring it out together. It takes the pressure off! The Spirit knows what he is doing and we're going to be looking to him to lead us.

You don't need to know much, and you certainly shouldn't wait until you feel like a spiritual giant. What you do need is the willingness to have a go, be real and take risks even though that means you may look and feel a bit foolish at times. If you think you can do that, you can do this!

It's a great idea to lead with a friend. The two of you can give each other encouragement, debrief after a group, pray for boldness together and laugh at each other's mistakes (that's what Mike does when Andy fails).

FOLLOWING THE SPIRIT

Planning is important - we don't want to presume on God or run the group as if it's an after-thought. At the same time, following the lead of the Spirit is of *primary* importance. He's the real group leader.

In practice this means we plan - there are group plans you can use as a basis in this booklet. However, it also means we are prepared to **be flexible with that plan**. This can be hard for those of us who are control freaks or completer-finishers (Andy is one of these in all walks of life. Mike is a food-based completer-finisher.) For those of us who like things structured and controlled, our attention can be on executing our plan; instead we need to see the main objective of the group as following the lead of the Spirit. This isn't to say that the Spirit isn't in our planning – he often is. However, a huge part of the purpose of the group is to invite the Spirit and attempt to follow his lead in the moment. We don't *need* to change the plan, but if it never changes it's possible we are missing something.

It's also likely that the group will look different week on week. The Spirit is endlessly creative. He usually does things differently. Andy's recent group had great fun following the Spirit's lead. As he prepared, Andy tried to ask the Lord each week 'What should it look like this time Lord?' At times things went as he had imagined beforehand, other times it seemed right that they should change direction. Sometimes they began with a time of worship and it seemed right to postpone the discussion and make space for the Spirit. Other times they worshipped, discussed and then prayed for people. Sometimes they chose a couple of people they particularly felt the Spirit highlight for the rest of the group to pray for. Other times it was as straightforward as asking who would like prayer to receive the Spirit, for healing or to receive the gift of tongues. The important thing isn't to be flexible for the sake of it, it's *to listen to the promptings of the Spirit* and see where you think he's taking you. Perhaps ask him throughout the day if there's anything particular he wants to do that evening. (For more on listening to God see chapters 7 and 8 on hearing God speak.) Bear in mind if you don't hear anything in particular it's a good idea to just use common sense!

The key point is: submit to the lead of the Holy Spirit and try to do what he is telling you.

BEING 'FAMILY'

An essential - but sometimes surprising - part of people growing in the things of the Spirit is the culture of the group. What do people feel like they are attending? Do people feel like they are coming together to study a book, complete a course, or to be a family? These differences in approach may seem small but they are actually worlds apart.

It's an obvious thing to say but when people are genuinely friends (not just making small talk) the potential to share honestly, be vulnerable and journey together is far greater. People rarely open up either to receive or to risk if they feel unsafe. You may want to give consideration as to how you are going to intentionally nurture family in the group. Sometimes we expect 'family' just to develop by showing up in the same room together, but this often isn't the case. How are you going to celebrate each other? How might you laugh together? What excuses can you find to eat together? How are you going to make it safe to fail when attempting to share a word of knowledge? How are you going to give people permission to admit they have doubts? How are you going to encourage and draw in those who are naturally shy and on the edge? How are you going to do this recognising that people's time is limited? This is not a culture that develops accidentally.

An important starting place is for you, the leader, to be clear that the purpose of the group is twofold:

1. To deepen the relationships people have with each other.
2. To grow in the things of the Spirit.

If you have these aims at the forefront of your mind when planning, leading and shaping the group, you will begin to move in the right direction. Some of it may be instinctive to us but in the best groups it will always be intentional.

BE ON YOUR GUARD

Resist any temptation to stifle or shy away from making space for God to move. We were once talking to a respected Christian leader, someone who has led a church into the things of the Spirit. He mentioned to us that he has never once stood up to invite the Spirit without the devil whispering in his ear, 'You don't need to do it this time. It would be easier not too. It's not that important.' We tend to hear that whisper and we imagine you will as well. The devil will suggest things like, 'If you invite the Spirit he probably won't turn up.' 'It's safer not to.' 'The Spirit came last week, he won't turn up this week.' 'Let's just have a really good discussion about this stuff, we don't actually need to do it.'

You will be most susceptible to these whispers when you are tired and feeling like a bit of a failure anyway so particularly be on your guard when you turn up to lead after a bad day. We'd encourage you to recognise them for the lies they are. Remember, the point of this group is to practice stepping out. Hear instead the voice of the Good Shepherd, our true Master, *"Ask and it will be given to you; seek and you will find; knock and the door will be opened to you… how much more will your Father in heaven give the Holy Spirit to those who ask him!"* Luke 11:9, 13. We usually keep in mind that the worst that can happen if we make space is that God doesn't do much and we go home early (and that's OK, we don't want to attempt to force things). The best that can happen is unbelievable breakthrough in someone's life. Given those stakes, it's worth taking the risk.

THE PRESSURE IS OFF

"I am the vine; you are the branches. If you remain in me and I in you, you will bear much fruit; apart from me you can do nothing." (John 15:5) It can be easy to read a booklet like this and think that the key to the Spirit moving is what we do. If that's what you think then you may find this quite a stressful few weeks!

We can't make the Spirit move. He blows where he wants. We can make space. We can prioritise following the lead of the Spirit. We can encourage a hunger for more of what God has for us. But God does what he wants, when he wants. We say this not to discourage you, but to encourage you. The branches of fruit trees don't stress or strain to produce fruit. They do so naturally because they are connected to the trunk. In the same way, we produce spiritual fruit by resting in Jesus, in his promises to send his Spirit and in his great desire to shower us with his mercy.

We don't want to underplay the role we have: it will be hard, we'll need to persevere through failure and we'll be flying-by-the-seat-of-our-pants at times. However, the pressure for this group to 'succeed' does not rest on us. Our role is to seek Jesus and to make space.

SUGGESTED READING PLAN

Everyday Supernatural has 12 chapters and we've included guides for every chapter except the Introduction and Chapter 5 which is a short introduction to the gifts of the Holy Spirit. We've also combined the two chapters on hearing God's voice into one week. This means there are nine week's worth of questions. Your timeframe may be shorter or longer but hopefully you can adapt the below. Obviously the more you can do, the better; we think all the chapters are important. However, if you are pressed for time we'd suggest you have a minimum of six sessions and see the below as chapters to definitely include:

Chapter 1	The Power is in the Presence
Chapter 2	Being Filled with the Spirit
Chapter 6	Praying in Tongues
Chapters 7 & 8	Hearing God Speak
Chapter 9	Praying for Healing
Chapter 10	For the Sake of the World

Suggested Questions:

We can't plan the worship, or the time you are going to make to wait on the Spirit and see what happens. We can, however, plan a few questions and some exercises that can be done outside of the group during the week. These exercises might seem a little 'token' or simplistic but they can make a dramatic difference.

CHAPTER 1

THE POWER IS IN THE PRESENCE

1. What particularly struck you when reading this chapter?

2. What do you understand by the phrase, 'the presence of God'?

3. Our relationship with God isn't based on feelings, but at the same time, many of us can speak of moments God has seemed especially close. Can you describe where/how you have experienced God's presence most keenly?

4. Moses, in a time of crisis, refused to leave God's presence (Exodus 33:15-16). David, though he could have sought many things, chased the 'one thing' of God's presence (Psalm 27:4-5). Why did they place such a priority on God's presence? What can we learn from them?

5. "Our goal should be relationship *with* Jesus, not power *from* Jesus." (Page 23) What might this look like in our lives?

6. "It's never been about what we can do – it's about *who we are with.*" (Page 26) What difference might this make when we look to pray for others?

At home...

Set aside a brief period of time (maybe 10 minutes) each day to 'practice the presence of God.' Identify a time and place you can do this regularly. It may be while you're doing the washing up or walking home, it might be sitting in your favourite chair. The important thing is deliberately and intentionally inviting God into the moment and choosing to become aware of his presence. Sometimes it can be helpful to do this first thing in the morning or last thing at night. You'll be amazed at what a difference just 10 minutes a day makes to our sensitivity to God's presence through the rest of the day.

CHAPTER 2

BEING FILLED WITH THE SPIRIT

1. What is the main thing you learned about the Holy Spirit from this chapter?

2. "To be a Christian isn't to tick a box next to a set of beliefs, it's to enter into a relationship with the living God. As we do this the living God pours his Spirit into us." (Page 38) Do you believe that you have received the Holy Spirit? Why/why not?

3. *"Therefore I want you to know that no one who is speaking by the Spirit of God says, "Jesus be cursed,' and no one can say, 'Jesus is Lord,' except by the Holy Spirit."* (1 Corinthians 12:3) Why is confessing 'Jesus is Lord' a sign of the Spirit living within us?

4. What did 'receiving the Holy Spirit' look like for the first believers? See Acts 2:1-13; 4:31; 10:44-48 and 19:6.

5. Paul writes to the Ephesians, *"Do not get drunk on wine, which leads to debauchery. Instead, be filled with the Spirit."* (Ephesians 5:18) The sense of this is that we are continuously filled with the Spirit. What might receiving more of the Spirit look like for you?

6. Mike and Andy suggest that three steps in our receiving more of the Spirit are:

> a. Accepting he is a gift given on the basis of Jesus' merit, not our own
> b. Persistently asking for more
> c. Trusting the giver (expressed as surrender and expectation)

Which of these steps is the biggest hurdle for you and why? How could you overcome this?

At home...

We're told by Paul to go on being filled with the Spirit. We're also told by Jesus to persistently seek things from God. Continue with your 10 minutes a day practising God's presence; as part of this time intentionally invite God to fill you again with his Holy Spirit.

CHAPTER 3

GOD'S POWER, OUR WEAKNESS

1. Was there anything that especially encouraged you in this chapter?

2. Many of us agree with the theory that 'God can use anyone,' but deep down we remain convinced that he only uses those who are strong and capable. Where do you think that subconscious belief has come from and why is it so deeply rooted?

3. The Bible is full of people who God used despite their brokenness. Why do you think God so consistently chose the seemingly weaker people to build his kingdom?

4. Lots of us seem to think that there is something about us that stops God using us. We don't pray enough, we are addicted to something, we are too fearful or shy, or we are caught up in destructive behaviour patterns. What would you say is one of your weaknesses, a barrier that you can't overcome and that you feel stops God using you?

5. Can you recall a time when you have stepped out, in weakness and vulnerability, because you thought God had spoken? What happened?

6. If we wait until we are 'sorted' we will be waiting forever. In what simple practical way would you like to begin to step out this week?

At home...

However you answered the last question, that's your challenge for the week! Identify where you feel weak and what growth would look like for you in this area, whether it's sharing the gospel, praying for a friend to be healed or asking God to fill someone with his Holy Spirit. Don't forget to keep up with your 10 minutes a day practising God's presence too.

CHAPTER 4

DO WHATEVER HE TELLS YOU

1. Jesus said, *"If you keep my commands, you will remain in my love, just as I have kept my Father's commands and remain in his love... You are my friends if you do what I command. I no longer call you servants, because a servant does not know his master's business. Instead, I have called you friends, for everything that I learned from my Father I have made known to you."* (John 14: 10, 14-15) Why is obedience the key to friendship with Jesus?

2. Have you ever had a time when you felt like God was asking you to 'step out of the boat'? How did you respond and what happened?

3. Jesus responded to Peter's doubt with kindness and help. What difference would it make to your ability to step out if you knew that no matter what happened, Jesus would respond to you with kindness?

4. Are there Christians you know where you can see the link between their obedience and their effectiveness in a certain area? What do you learn from how they live?

5. God 'doesn't wait until it's convenient, comfortable or safe' (page 84) before asking us to do things. How might this change the ways in which we listen to him?

6. Is there anything you think God is specifically asking you to do in the immediate future? What is it and are you going to do it?

At home...

As part of your daily 10 minutes with the Lord, ask him if there is a particular way he wants you to obey him that day. Listen for his answer... and then do it! You will be amazed after a little while – God really will speak to you.

CHAPTER 6

PRAYING IN TONGUES

1. What particularly struck you when reading this chapter?

2. Speaking in tongues is no more a status symbol than having blue eyes. It can, however, be very encouraging to hear other people's stories. Has anyone in the group received the gift of tongues? How did it happen?

3. Read 1 Corinthians 14 verses 1-5 and 13-19. Paul is addressing a misuse of the gift of tongues here. What you can learn about Paul's own use of tongues? Does anything stand out to you?

4. Whilst the gift of tongues is not the most important of the gifts, it can be a phenomenally helpful way of praying. Paul writes, *"If I pray in a tongue, my spirit prays, but my mind is unfruitful. So what shall I do? I will pray with my spirit, but I will also pray with my understanding; I will sing with my spirit, but I will also sing with my understanding."* (1 Corinthians 14:14-15). What is meant by 'praying' or 'singing' with the Spirit?

5. Praying in tongues is one way that we pray in the Spirit. Mike and Andy talk about how the gift of tongues:

- Gives 'words for the soul'
- Helps us draw near to God
- Helps us see kingdom break-throughs

Which of these three things excites you? Why?

6. We can frequently doubt that God wants to give us good things – like the gift of tongues. What might give us confidence and expectation as we seek this gift?

Ministry time note:

In this session you may want to make space to pray for people to receive the gift. Not everyone will want to; for some this will be very new and they may want time to process the teaching first. It's important to be sensitive to that. However, for those who would like to receive the gift of tongues, it can be helpful to remember the three steps mentioned on pages 105-6: believe, ask, step out. In addition it's important to stress how *normal* praying in tongues feels; it is not divine ventriloquism, but an act of collaboration.

When praying for people to receive the gift of tongues we often do the following:

- Identify who would like to receive the gift
- Invite the Holy Spirit
- All begin to praise God in English

- Invite all those who already pray in tongues to begin to pray in their prayer language
- Invite and encourage those who want to begin to step out and start to pray. They will feel foolish and it's important they are reassured that it is a safe place and reminded that if it's gobbledygook, let it be gobbledygook for the Lord.
- Encourage and affirm what the Spirit is doing

At home...

If you already speak in tongues or have received the gift during this session, practice using this gift daily. It may be helpful to identify a time or place (a car journey, a walk to school, the shower) where you know you'll be able to practice regularly.

If you haven't yet received the gift of tongues but would like to, continue to ask God and attempt to step out again.

CHAPTER 7 & 8

HEARING GOD SPEAK

1. Can you describe a time that when you remember God clearly speaking to you? (It could have been through something very normal, e.g. scripture, a sermon, a friend, or through a prophetic word etc)

2. God often seems to speak to us in riddles; why might this be?

3. Read 1 Corinthians 14:1-6. In what ways does prophecy build up the church? Have you seen or experienced this?

4. Prophecy involves revelation, interpretation and application. What do these three elements mean? How would you describe them?

5. Mike and Andy list a number of the gentle ways that we receive revelation:

- SEE - visions, screen of mind
- FEEL - physical or emotional
- SPEAK - automatic mouth
- HEAR - a thought that's not your thought
- KNOW - a sudden conviction of something

Which of these can you most connect with?

6. How might you practice prophecy this week?

Ministry time note:
This session is a great opportunity to practice prophecy. One simple way to do this might be for you to choose one or two people to pray for. Invite the Holy Spirit and encourage the rest of the group to listen to anything they feel the Lord is saying for that person. Then encourage them to step out by sharing it. It's always helpful to:

- Make sure people feel safe to get it wrong
- Remind people that God usually speaks very gently; we're often not sure until after we've shared it
- Lower the bar. This isn't about knowing someone's passport number – what might seem like a simple word to you might mean a great deal to the person you are praying for.
- Don't overthink it! It doesn't matter how simple or strange it seems, just go for it.
- Remember that prophecy is for strengthening, encouraging and comforting people and we should be mindful of this when sharing

At home...

Take every opportunity to listen to God for other people this week. If you regularly pray for certain people you may want to ask God for a Bible verse or word of encouragement to give to them. If you are praying for a particular situation, ask God for a word of wisdom. Challenge yourself to give a word of knowledge to someone.

CHAPTER 9

PRAYING FOR HEALING

1. Have you, or someone you've prayed for, ever experienced physical or emotional healing? What happened?

2. *Why* we pray matters. Jesus' prayers were clearly motivated by compassion (Matthew 14:14). How might our willingness to pray and our manner of praying differ if compassion were our primary motivation?

3. A lack of sensitivity when praying for healing can damage people. It can also be easy for us to pick up all sorts of distracting or unhelpful practices. What basic principles can help us avoid this?

4. "No one "earns" healing anymore than anyone can "earn" salvation. Jesus paid the price so we wouldn't have to." (Page 162) How does this affect the way we pray for healing?

5. Mike and Andy suggest a model of:
   - *Remembering* who is responsible
   - *Asking* what hurts

- *Following* the lead of the Spirit in how to pray
- *Checking in*
- *Following up* by making sure the person knows they are loved

What is the most helpful piece of advice you have received when learning to pray for healing?

6. "When it comes to healing, the best way to learn is by doing." (Page 179) If you have never done this before, how will you begin to practice praying for healing? If you are more experienced, what is a 'next step' you can challenge yourself to take?

At home...

Commit to praying every day for someone who is sick. If it is appropriate, offer to pray for them in person. Be sure to ask towards the end of the week if they have noticed any improvement.

CHAPTER 10

FOR THE SAKE OF THE WORLD

1. Have you had any experience of praying for healing or sharing a prophetic word with someone who is not a Christian? How did it go?

2. The Bible tells us we are sent with the authority of Jesus (Matthew 28:18-20), and the power of the Spirit (Acts 1:8), *in order to witness.*

In what ways have you experienced the Spirit partnering with you as you look to reach someone? What does this look like in everyday life?

3. Praying for strangers is clearly part of the everyday supernatural, but how might it become a part of our *existing relationships* with family, friends and colleagues? What might this look like for you?

4. Mike and Andy write of their friend who says his success comes down to expectation, not gifting (pages 198-199). How would you

approach your days/conversations differently if you shared this confident expectation that God was going to use you?

5. The early church prayed not just for supernatural signs but for supernatural boldness. Have you ever persistently sought God for boldness? What happened?

6. Mike and Andy talk about their own journeys of growing into this. What could be a first step for you?

At home...

Share your faith in some form this week. This can be as simple as offering to pray for someone who is not a Christian. Don't just pick someone at random, be attentive to anyone who God is highlighting to you.

CHAPTER 11

GROWING IN FAITH

1. What particularly stood out to you when reading this chapter?

2. Very few of us ever feel like we have 'enough' faith. Why is this? In what ways does this restrict us?

3. "Faith is really about two things: trusting God's character, and stepping out because of this trust."(Page 210) In what ways (either in the Bible or in your life) has God shown he is trustworthy?

4. In Mark 9:14-29 a father brings his demonised son to Jesus. He tells Jesus, *"I do believe; help me overcome my unbelief!"* How might Jesus answer that prayer? How might he grow your faith?

5. "A life of faith isn't one free from all doubt, it's one where we keep expecting God to be faithful in the midst of our questions." (Page 209) Describe a time when you've had to trust God in the midst of difficult circumstances. What was the result of that time on your relationship with God?

6. Just as a muscle grows when it is exercised, so faith grows as we step out. In what way would you like to begin to step out more? What might be a possible 'faith exercise' that you could do?

At home...

Find a way to step out in an area that you want to grow your faith in. That could be anything from praying for healing, to sharing a prophecy, or reaching out to someone even though it feels like a risk. Faith grows as it is exercised – do some exercise and report back to the group!

CHAPTER 12

SUSTAINING THE SUPERNATURAL

1. What is the key lesson God has taught you during the weeks we've been looking at *Everyday Supernatural*?

2. "Success in the everyday supernatural isn't about getting e v e r y-thing right; it's about keeping going." (Page 225) What are the main things that could stop you from keeping going? How might you address them?

3. James 1:2-4 says, *"Consider it pure joy, my brothers and sisters, whenever you face trials of many kinds, because you know that the testing of your faith produces perseverance. Let perseverance finish its work so that you may be mature and complete, not lacking anything."*

Perseverance can only develop in a time of testing. What difference might this make to the way you approach challenges?

4. "If we make the decision to plod today, in fifty years time we'll be rejoicing that we did!" (Page 229) When you are in your old age what do you want to be able to look back and say about how you followed God?

5. Andy and Mike talk about 'sowing seeds'. What seeds have you sown recently? How do you do this best?

6. Intimacy with the Lord is key to growing in the everyday supernatural. What habits do you want to continue to develop that might help you draw close to God?

At home...

What one manageable and achievable practice could help you stay close to Jesus in the long haul? Do this!

We'd love to hear about your journey as you've followed this guide! You can email **testimonies@soulsurvivor.com** to tell us your story.

LEADING A MINISTRY TIME

Believing that the ministry and gifts of the Holy Spirit are for today and making space for the Holy Spirit to actually move don't automatically follow on from each other. There can be a number of reasons for this but often it's because we lack the confidence to step out and give it a go. Here we want to demystify what it means to lead a ministry time and talk through some simple steps in the hope of demonstrating that anyone can do it. This is something we do in relationship with God and in dependence on *him,* not on techniques. However, we can offer principles that we hope will guide you as you look to grow in this area. It should be noted that these principles apply at a small group level, but they are just as important when leading a larger gathering as well.

1. GIVING UP CONTROL

Let's be honest, many of us are control freaks. This isn't necessarily a bad thing when leading a small group. It is good and important to be prepared. We want to have fun, we want to have a meaningful time of worship and Bible study, and we want to eat restaurant quality food. (Mike, on principle, only attends groups *in* restaurants). However, if we're not careful, all of this can cause us to shut down any contribution that hasn't had prior approval. Of course the Holy Spirit is present and can inspire and guide us in our preparation but, we suggest, there is something utterly biblical and excellently power-ful in inviting him to move upon us and then giving him the space and time to do so. This involves an element of giving up control. In practice it means we arrive prepared but that throughout the meeting we should be constantly seeking to discern what God might be doing. We will need to be willing to put our prepared contributions on hold if it seems that he wants to intervene. When God takes over, people often become deeply aware of his loving presence, not as an intellectual theory but as a living reality. People will often experience healing in their bodies, minds or emotions. In our experience, whilst we can't manufacture these moments, they are wonderful and not to be missed when they do happen. It can be helpful to recognise that leading a ministry time does not mean, 'leading a slot at the end of a service.' It can mean this, but it is much broader. It's more a case of, when the Spirit starts to move, how do we follow? Giving up control is the starting place for this.

2. CONSTANTLY ASKING

How does this happen in practice? Throughout the meeting we are asking the Lord if there is anything he wants to say or do which is not part of our agenda. Asking God what he wants to do isn't something that starts in a specific ministry time, it is an attitude that we want to maintain as much as possible, and it's the attitude that allows for ministry times to happen at any moment.

During the meeting and especially during times of worship it can be very helpful to look around the room to see what the Father is doing. We are looking for indications that the Holy Spirit is touching people's hearts, healing them, or meeting with them in some other way. These indications may be minor, for example, someone looking very peaceful or someone beginning to cry. There may be something more dramatic that begins to happen. If someone particularly catches our attention we find it helpful to ask God, 'What are you doing in that person?' 'Is that just for them or is that for others?' At other times, we may not see anything obvious in a person but there might be 'heaviness' in the room, or a silence that seems 'pregnant' with God's presence. This could be because of all that restaurant quality food and the fact that it's 9.30pm. It might be something more, however, and the important thing is not to rush past these moments. It's to make space and engage with God to see if he is up to something. It's important to recognise that with this constant attitude of asking, we are not trying to manufacture anything; it is perfectly fine to just move on to the next item if nothing much is going on. What we are doing is paying attention.

3. MAKING SPACE

At our church, Soul Survivor Watford, we always make space for ministry at the end of the service after the teaching. We believe the preaching of the Word should invite a response from those listening. Of course the response should be outworked in an ongoing way in our daily lives. However, there should also be a place for people to respond in an appropriate way there and then and seek the empowering, help or comfort of the Holy Spirit so that as a result they can live differently. The response may be in the form of a greater commitment to follow Jesus in a particular area, it may be to receive and know in greater measure the grace and love of God, it may be that the teaching has unearthed a realisation of sinful actions or attitudes that need repenting of. We always want to make space for people to receive prayer for these things. We also want to make time as part of our service for people who come burdened, or sick in body or mind, or anxious over a life decision they have to make, to receive prayer.

We value the worship of God, so we will never have a service when we don't give time to worship. We value the preaching of the Word so we will always have a talk. We value the ministry and leading of the Holy Spirit, so we also always make time for that. We always begin the ministry before we close the service as this is an important part of our meeting. We don't send those who want prayer over to the side or to another room, they come to the front. Again, this is because we want everyone to know that we believe this is important and valuable and want openness to the Holy Spirit to be part of our church culture and not something reserved for the keen or the needy. We also invite people to come forward for a very practical reason. It is much easier to see who needs prayer and to direct people to them when they're at the front. For some it is also important that they make a conscious step to say they want prayer and are seeking to meet with God; coming forward can say this in a symbolic way. This principle very much applies in your small group. Ministry times are often squeezed out by all the other important things we want to fit into our allotted time. Make the ministry time a main event, a significant feature of what you are going to do as a group not an optional extra.

4. WAIT

Every time we invite the Holy Spirit to move among us, we will wait. And wait. And wait a little more. We cannot over emphasise the importance of waiting. So many of us find this very hard to do but we have discovered it is the key to seeing God move in power. The longer we wait, often, the more he does!

The temptation for many of us (especially those of us who are evangelicals!) is to kill a ministry time with words. Often we need to simply shut up and let God be God. We don't need to pray long-winded prayers. Simply invite the Spirit to come and then give him space to do so. We must also resist the temptation to hype up the atmosphere. (Those of us who are charismatic Pentecostals can feel particularly tempted to do this!) We don't need a particular type of music to be playing for God to move or to goad people into making an emotional response. We kill the religion and wait. The Holy Spirit will sometimes move in great power and sometimes more gently. When less happens, we just go home earlier! When we manipulate an atmosphere or hype a response, we simply lose credibility.

Sometimes, after waiting for a while, there may be an obvious response. On other occasions, the response may be very gentle but we become aware that God is meeting with people. We may invite those who are aware that the Holy Spirit is resting on them to stand up, and encourage those around to lay hands on them and join in with what God has already begun to do. On other occasions, it will be appropriate to invite those who are sensing God meeting with them to take a step forward or respond in some other way.

On occasion the Lord may give you some words of knowledge, prophetic insight into the state of individual lives and what he wants to do. If that happens, speak the words out, humbly and gently and invite a response.

The idea isn't that we become the centre of attention, we simply focus on Jesus. Avoid theatrics at all costs. Often we're not sure what God is doing and it is rare that we are completely clear what he is saying. It is better to go for it anyway and if we get it wrong, it really doesn't matter. If we wait for certainty, we will probably wait forever. Don't feel you have to become overly spiritual; aim to be 'naturally supernatural'. Remember, it is surprising how 'unspiritual' spiritual gifts feel.

5. PASTOR

Ministry may be new to many people and so it is wise to think about everyone in the group and what their expectations are and their previous experience has been. As the leader, it is your job to pastor the group. A large part of this will involve explaining (as much as possible) what is happening. It can be helpful to state what you are going to be doing as this gives people context and it helps them relax and feel safe. For example, if you are about to make space and invite the Holy Spirit, tell people. Stress that there's no need for anyone to do anything religious, explain you are all going to wait and give it some time. Make the point that no one needs to force this, either God will do it or he won't.

As and when God begins to move you will need to play-it-by-ear but you will need to explain, explain, explain! The great Corinthian heresy when it came to the ministry of the Holy Spirit and the use of the gifts of the Spirit was that it involved a super-spiritual exclusive club. 'Outsiders' or visitors were left out. We sometimes see this today in so-called charismatic churches. We can fall into a 'secret' language or a way of responding that only the spiritual 'in-crowd' can understand. This is incredibly destructive to community and must be actively avoided. Our role as leaders is to keep everyone together, to explain and reassure. This means that we should always be asking ourselves, "What might those on the fringe be thinking now?" Then as pastors we gently address those questions.

Sometimes there may be a strong human response to the activity of the Holy Spirit. Some folk may weep, others laugh, others shake or even fall down and rest in God's presence. The temptation at that point is to think, "Everyone else is meeting with God, what is wrong with me? Why have I been left out?" So we will say something like; "If you are not feeling anything, it's OK, neither are we (as usually we don't feel anything!). There is nothing wrong with you."

Some might be wondering, "What on earth is going on? Are people making it up and getting hysterical?" We may say something like; "Is what you're seeing and hearing all God? No. It is our response to God. Some of us are more naturally emotional so we are more likely to respond in that way. Some of us are more aware of our bodies and so we are more likely to respond to the Holy Spirit's activity in a physical way. Some of us are more cerebral and so we will probably respond in a more intellectual way. Let's give ourselves space to be different. No one has to do what anyone else is doing. The crying you hear is probably only pain being released in the Father's presence. The laughing you hear is probably simply a response to a deeper realisation of the Father's love." And so on. People feel safe and included when they realise that we understand their questions and concerns and are attempting to answer them. If something especially dramatic begins to happen with an individual then things can be quite messy. There's no need to be afraid of mess but you will want to make sure you protect the dignity of the individual and that they are loved and cared for. When someone is being prayed for, if they leave knowing nothing else, they should at least leave knowing they've been loved.

6. EVERYONE CAN PLAY

A final but absolutely vital thing to be aware of is that anyone can do this. The goal is not that the leaders do ministry at the rest of the group, it's that we make space to meet the Lord together. Some will be more experienced at praying than others and if that is the case then encourage these people to coach and support those for whom this is new. The purpose of the group is that people are equipped to do these things, not that they come simply to be ministered to. Keep looking to encourage people to step out and pray for each other. If you aren't sure what the Lord is doing then listen to him together and see what others are sensing. Resist the temptation to make it about you; it's about Jesus' people being released to do the work of ministry. At best we are facilitators for that. The difficulty with writing this is that while we can give certain principles for leading ministry times that we have learned, we must emphasise that there is no blueprint. It really is about learning to listen to the Holy Spirit and seeing what he is doing, both with our natural eyes and our spiritual eyes. As is often the case when we step out, we feel vulnerable and we are dependent on God showing up.

To sum up: be bold, be kind, be humble and you won't go far wrong. Give it a go and then persevere. Our churches need to have their minds renewed by the teaching of God's truth and their hearts warmed and healed as the Holy Spirit fills them with the revelation of the love of the Father for them. Step out, wait on God and see what he wants to do.

FURTHER INFO

Find out more about our Naturally Supernatural summer and winter conferences at **www.naturallysupernatural.co.uk** which are all about equipping us to live the Spirit-led life. You'll also find related blogs on our website as well as teaching from previous events that you can watch for free.

Connect on social media and stay up to date with the latest Naturally Supernatural news – we're NSNconf on Facebook, Instagram and Twitter.

Naturally Supernatural is part of Soul Survivor. Find out more at **www.soulsurvivor.com**

NOTES

CHAPTER 2

1. "Quenching the Spirit", *The Westminster Record*, September 1964, quoted in David Watson, *One in the Spirit* (London: Hodder & Stoughton, 1973), 70.

2. Thomas A. Smail, *Reflected Glory: The Spirit in Christ and Christians* (London: Hodder Christian paperbacks), 1975, 107.

3. Watson, *One in the Spirit*, 24.

4. Martyn Lloyd-Jones, quoted in Nicky Gumbel, *Alpha: Questions of Life* (Eastbourne: Kingsway, 2007), 147.

CHAPTER 6

1. David Pytches, *Come Holy Spirit* (London: Hodder & Stoughton, 1995), 53.

2. Pytches, *Come Holy Spirit*, 54, adapted.

3. R.A. Torrey, *The Power of Prayer and the Prayer of Power* (Newberry, FL: Bridge Logos, 2009), 90–91.

4. Jackie Pullinger, quoted in Nicky Gumbel, *Alpha: Questions of Life* (Eastbourne: Kingsway, 2007), 151.

CHAPTER 7

1. Richard Foster, *Celebration of Discipline* (London: Hodder & Stoughton, 2008), 97. Foster's chapter on solitude is excellent for anyone wanting to look at this in more detail.

CHAPTER 8

1. Michael Green, *To Corinth with Love* (London: Hodder & Stoughton, 1982), 75, quoted in David Pytches, *Come Holy Spirit* (London: Hodder & Stoughton, 1995), 66.

2. Simon Ponsonby, *More* (Colorado Springs, CO: David C Cook, 2004), 102.

3. Ponsonby, *More*, 102.

4. John Wimber, *Power Evangelism* (London: Hodder & Stoughton, 2001), 76.

5. Ponsonby, *More*, 102.

CHAPTER 9

1. C.S. Lewis, *Letters to Malcolm: Chiefly on Prayer*, accessed online on 24 March 2016, http://www.goodreads.com/quotes/178974-novelty-may-fix-our-attention -not-even-on-the-service.

2. Nicky Gumbel, *Alpha: Questions of Life* (Eastbourne: Kingsway, 2007), 198.

CHAPTER 10

1. We have changed the neighbour's name.

CHAPTER 11

1. Frederick William Danker, ed., *A Greek-English Lexicon of the New Testament and Other Early Christian Literature* (Chicago: University of Chicago Press, 1979), 444.

2. C. H. Spurgeon, sermon "The Sad Wonder," accessed online 11 March 2016, http://www.spurgeongems.org/vols16-18/chs935.pdf.

3. George Stormont, *Smith Wigglesworth: A Man Who Walked with God* (Tulsa, OK: Harrison House Publishers, 1989), 60.

4. Stormont, *Wigglesworth*, 47.

5. Brennan Manning, *Ruthless Trust* (Nashville: Harper Paperbacks, 2001), 5.

6. Quoted in Brené Brown, *Rising Strong* (London: Vermilion), 7.

CHAPTER 12

1. Dietrich Bonhoeffer, *The Cost of Discipleship*, accessed online on 30 March 2016, https://www.goodreads.com/quotes/98256-when-christ-calls-a-man-he-bids-him -come-and.

2. Thomas A. Smail, *Reflected Glory: The Spirit in Christ and Christians* (London: Hodder and Stoughton, 1975), 116.

3. "War Crimes," *The West Wing*, season 3, episode 6, directed by Alex Graves, first aired 7 November 2001 (Burbank, CA: Warner Home Video), DVD.

4. www.goodreads.com/quotes/44552-yesterday-is-gone-tomorrow-has-not-yet-come-we -have.